Fatherhood Arrested

Parenting from Within the Juvenile Justice System

Anne Nurse

Vanderbilt University Press
Nashville

This book is printed on acid-free paper.
Manufactured in the United States of America

Library of Congress Cataloging-in-Publication Data

Nurse, Anne, 1968–
Fatherhood arrested : parenting from within the juvenile justice
system / Anne Nurse.— 1st ed.
     p. cm.
Includes bibliographical references and index.
     ISBN 0-8265-1404-9 (cloth : alk. paper)
     ISBN 0-8265-1405-7 (paper : alk. paper)
     1. Juvenile delinquents—Rehabilitation—United States. 2.
Juvenile parole—United States. 3. Teenage fathers—
Rehabilitation-United States. 4. Absentee fathers—
Rehabilitation—United States. 5.Parenting—Study and teaching—
United States. 6. Children of prisoners—United States. 7. Father
and child—United States. I. Title.
HV9104 .N87 2002
362.82'95—dc21

                                        2002001704

Part of chapter 2 appeared as an article entitled "The Structure of
the Juvenile Prison: Constructing the Inmate Father" in *Youth and
Society* 32 (2001): 360–94. © 2001 by Sage Publications. It is
reprinted with permission of Sage Publications.

Sections of chapters 3 and 4 are drawn from the article "Coming
Home: The Transition from Incarcerated to Paroled Young Father,"
which appeared in *Families, Crime, and Criminal Justice:
Contemporary Perspectives in Family Research,* vol. 2, ed. Greer
Litton Fox and Michael L. Benson (2000). It is reprinted with the
permission of Elsevier Press.

To John

Contents

Acknowledgments

I would like to thank the paroled fathers who shared their lives with me. I know that many agreed to participate in this project because they wanted to help other young men like themselves. I hope that this book does justice to their time and effort. I would also like to thank the parole agents and staff at the California Youth Authority. Their help made this project possible. Many thanks to the amazing women who helped me conduct surveys: Gina, Leslie, Amina, Sol, Kathy, Barbara, and Patricia. On the days I was ready to give up, their good-natured willingness to drive endless hours, to hang around and wait for interviews in fast-food restaurants, and to listen with empathy kept me going.

A number of people helped with drafts of this book. Special thanks to Mary Jackman, Carole Joffe, Lawrence Cohen, James Cramer, Mary Ann Mason, and three anonymous reviewers for giving generously of their time and wisdom. I appreciate Michael Ames at Vanderbilt for his belief in the book and for his constant reminders to write about people, not data. Thanks to Ann Whetzel and Matt Nelson for spending many hours checking the accuracy of the details and citations. Finally, my eternal gratitude to my mother, who copyedited far too many versions of this book. Her support and patience was integral to the project.

This research could not have happened without the generous support of three granting agencies: the National Science Foundation (Dissertation Improvement Award no. SBR-9633153), the U.S. Department of Justice (OJP-97-017-M), and the Ford Foundation (#975-1299).

1

Prison and Fatherhood
Overlapping Social Problems

In recent years there has been much attention focused on economically disadvantaged young men. Two issues, crime and out-of-wedlock fathering, have caused public anxiety and political debate. A perception of rampant criminal activity and irresponsible fathering has fueled welfare reform proposals, criminal law reforms, and changes to the child support system. The two issues have been discussed separately, but little attention has been paid to the fact that these social problems intersect.

Nationally, about 5 percent of men father a child before their twentieth birthday and another 8 percent do so between the ages of 20 and 24 (Darroch, Landry, and Oslak 1999). Few states keep accurate counts of juvenile fathers in prison, but the existing counts indicate that the number is high. In California, for example, the juvenile prison system has data suggesting that over 25 percent of its inmates are fathers (California Youth Authority 1995). In Ohio the statistics are similar; a study conducted by the Department of Youth Services estimates that 22.4 percent of their inmates are fathers (Abeyratne, Sowards, and Brewer 1995).

One of the primary reasons for the overrepresentation of fathers in juvenile prison is that incarceration and out-of-wedlock fathering are concentrated in the same poor and minority communities. Figures from 1999 indicate that while 368 of every 100,000 juveniles in the general population are in custody on any given day, the rate among blacks and Latinos is much higher. For every 100,000 black juveniles, 1,018 are incarcerated (OJJDP 1999). As a result of this high incarceration rate, it is estimated that one-third of all black males in their twenties are under the supervision of the correctional system (Mauer and Huling 1995). Latinos also have high rates of incarceration; for every 100,000 Latino juveniles, 515 are in custody (OJJDP 1999). In 1995, minorities made up about 32 percent of the juvenile population but constituted 68 percent of those in secure detention centers (Sickmund, Snyder, and Poe-Yamagata 1997).

Research suggests that the overrepresentation of blacks and Latinos in prison is primarily a result of discrimination and poverty. While black youth exhibit more delinquent behavior than white youth, and both blacks and Latinos have a slightly higher involvement in index crimes,[1] these differences are small and generally fail to reach statistical significance (Huizinga and Elliott 1987). Race and ethnicity do appear to play an important role in decisions made by police, judges, and courts (Bishop and Frazier 1996; Conley 1994; Wordes, Bynum, and Corley 1994). As a result of these decisions, minorities are more likely than whites to serve time in prison, even when the severity of the crime and the defendant's past record are taken into account. In the United States, race and ethnicity are also highly correlated with poverty. Blacks and Latinos tend to be poorer than whites and less able to afford lawyers and alternatives to prison, such as private treatment centers (Bishop and Frazier 1996; Bortner and Williams 1997).

The disproportionate incarceration of young blacks and Latinos ensures that many fathers end up behind bars. Black men between the ages of fifteen and nineteen father children at over twice the rate of whites (17.5 births per 1,000 white men per year as compared with 41.5 for blacks). The disparity between groups drops only slightly between the ages of twenty and twenty-four, when we see 76.8 per 1,000 white men fathering children as compared with 133.5 black men (Ventura et al. 2001, 48). Latinos have a birthrate that is comparable to the rate for blacks (Ventura et al. 2001, 10).

The intersection of race/ethnicity, poverty, and young parenthood leads to an overrepresentation of fathers in the juvenile prison population. This overrepresentation is further pronounced by the fact that fathers, regardless of their backgrounds, appear to be more likely than their nonfather counterparts to engage in delinquent behaviors and to go to prison (Christmon and Lucky 1994; Elster, Lamb, and Tavare 1987; Lerman 1993; Thornberry et al. 2000). In a large-scale study of the relationship between delinquency and young fatherhood, Stouthamer-Loeber and Wei (1998) found that fathers are more than twice as likely to engage in delinquent behaviors as are nonfathers. The fathers are also more likely to abuse alcohol and drugs, be disruptive in school, and exhibit aggressive behaviors. In their conclusion, Stouthamer-Loeber and Wei comment: "Compared to males of the same neighborhood, race, and age, young fathers tended to be troubled young men who were significantly more likely than their matched controls to have engaged in varied serious acts of delinquency in the year of fatherhood and in the year after" (64).

Social Implications of Incarcerated Fathers

The incarceration rates for young men have increased dramatically during the past two decades. The period from 1983 to 1995, for example, saw an increase in juvenile incarceration of almost 50 percent. In the mid-1990s, there were more than 86,000 young men in public and private correctional institutions, camps, and treatment centers nationwide (Sickmund, Snyder, and Poe-Yamagata 1997). Although juvenile arrests for both violent and property crimes have dropped in the past five years, we cannot expect to see an immediate impact on prison population statistics. In 1997, the U.S. House of Representatives passed a bill authorizing the distribution of $1.6 billion to states that toughen penalties for juvenile offenders. These changes to the juvenile laws will likely result in the incarceration of a greater number of young people for longer periods of time. If the juvenile prison population continues to grow nationwide, more and more young fathers will spend some part of their children's lives behind bars. A failure to recognize this overlap between prison and young fatherhood has serious and wide-ranging social consequences.

The incarceration of large numbers of young fathers has a profound impact on the children, women, and communities with which they are associated. While in some cases incarceration's impact is positive—when, for example, an abusive father is removed from a home—research suggests that the impact is more often negative. Women and children left behind must contend with the financial pressure caused by a loss of support from the father. Even fathers not legally employed before incarceration may have been supporting children through illegal or off-the-books income. Those women and children who rely on support from fathers are often forced to change homes or to go on public assistance when this support is withdrawn (Davis 1992). In surveys, the wives and girlfriends of incarcerated men report that their most difficult struggles are financial (Ferraro et al. 1983).

Women and children also report emotional difficulties, including loneliness and social stigmatization, resulting from the incarceration of the father. Research has found that such children often exhibit symptoms that include nightmares, depression, and poor achievement (Johnston and Gabel 1995). Mothers report negative behavioral changes in their children after the father goes to prison (Fritsch and Burkhead 1981). Incarceration strains the relationship between a father and his children and between a father and the mother of his children. Incarcerated men miss years of their children's lives and often become estranged from them. Children grow and change rapidly, and it is extremely difficult to maintain a close relationship from a distance (McDermott and King 1992). Imprisoned men also miss years of their wives' and girlfriends' lives, and they can only provide them with limited emotional support. As a result, incarceration is linked to high rates of divorce between inmates and the mothers of their children (Hairston 1995). Children are further stressed by divorce and the subsequent introduction of new men into the mothers' lives. The association between prison and family dissolution is particularly disturbing given evidence showing that strong family relations may be the key to helping men make a successful transition out of prison. Specifically, men who develop strong bonds with their children and other family members appear to have lower levels of postrelease depression (Ekland-Olson et al. 1983) and lower rates of recidivism (Hughes 1998; Sampson and Laub 1993).

The concentration of incarceration in poor and minority communities contributes to poverty and other social problems. Losing potential wage earners, through high incarceration rates, increases poverty levels in these neighborhoods. Incarcerated men's families are often forced to turn to their relatives or to the public assistance system for financial help (Bakker, Morris, and Janus 1978; Davis 1992). The result is that poverty and welfare use become further concentrated in communities with high levels of economic distress. At the same time, these communities have fewer available male role models for children and fewer eligible marriage partners for women.

Current Public Policy toward
Young Incarcerated Fathers

Few public policies address the myriad social problems associated with the incarceration of young fathers. Instead, we have one set of policies for young fathers and another for juvenile delinquents. The problem is that, for incarcerated fathers, the two sets of policy are often in direct conflict. While both fatherhood policy and criminal policy emphasize individual responsibility, fatherhood policy is designed to encourage men to take responsibility for their children whereas criminal policy seeks to encourage responsible behavior by imposing maximum penalties on juvenile offenders. Young criminal fathers are caught in the middle of these policies. Their lengthy prison terms make it impossible for them to fulfill their parenting duties.

Our current juvenile delinquency policy is determined, in large part, by public anxiety about crime. Public pressure has encouraged state legislatures to increase the sentence length of offenders and, at the same time, to reduce their privileges. As a result, politicians latch on to "get tough on crime" measures as an effective way to win elections. From a political standpoint, criminals are particularly useful scapegoats for social ills because they can be blamed for their own predicament (Sabo, Kupers, and London 2001).

Current fatherhood policy, with its emphasis on the importance of father participation, is motivated by a somewhat different set of financial and ideological concerns from those driving incarceration policy. On a fiscal level, fatherhood policies are designed to save taxpayers money by limiting the number of single mothers on public assistance. The intent is to increase the amount of child support that single mothers receive from the fathers of their children. If successful, the number of women who need public assistance could be reduced. An example of this type of policy is the requirement that women who apply for Aid to Families with Dependent Children identify the fathers of their children. Once they do so, the fathers can be tracked down and served with child support orders. Another law, designed to ensure that men actually pay child support, mandates that the payments be deducted automatically from a father's paycheck.

While the primary goal of our public policy regarding fathers is fiscal, there are other motivations as well. A 1997 public education campaign in California illustrates the state's dedication to eliciting a range of participation from young fathers. Various billboards appeared that featured young fathers holding babies. In some, the text read, "Fatherhood Is Forever," and in others, "Being a Father Means Being There." At the same time, the state aired television advertisements with similar themes. California has also been at the forefront of a movement to provide parenting skills classes to young men. A pilot program in 1997 allowed 26 counties to provide such classes to young men in alternative schools, juvenile halls, and regular high schools. The goal of these classes, and of the billboard and television campaign, was to encourage young men's active involvement with their children.

This Study

Given the social implications and policy contradictions raised by incarcerated and paroled fathers, an increase in our understanding of their lives and attitudes is important. Such knowledge will help in the formulation of appropriate and consistent policy responses. This book looks at paroled fathers in the Northern Region of the California Youth Authority (CYA). The region extends from Bakersfield to the Oregon border and is responsible for about half of the state's inmates and parolees. The CYA is the agency assigned to supervise the most serious and repeat juvenile offenders in California. To fulfill this function, the agency runs eleven prisons, four camps, two residential drug treatment centers, and sixteen parole offices. In 1995, approximately nine thousand people, ages thirteen to twenty-five, were housed in CYA institutions; six thousand more were on parole (CYA 1996). Among all states, California had the largest number of admissions to juvenile facilities (Austin et al. 1995).

My involvement with the CYA began in the spring of 1995, when I was hired as part of a team to evaluate the parenting classes then being provided for some of the paroled fathers. The juvenile system in California, similar to those in other states, allows inmates to be paroled from prison before their sentences are complete. The decision to release a youth to parole is made by a seven-member board, appointed by the governor. Once an inmate is released, he or she must meet regularly with an agent and abide by a set of restrictions determined by the Board of Parole. These restrictions specify both activities to avoid (e.g., drug or alcohol use; associating with gang members) and activities that are required (attending school, seeking work, or participating in parenting classes). Any violation of these conditions can result in a parolee being returned to prison to serve out his or her sentence. While all juvenile inmates and parolees in California committed their crimes before the age of eighteen, they can remain under CYA parole supervision until they are twenty-five years old.

It was with a degree of trepidation that I attended my first parenting class. To my relief, I was accepted and the young men were friendly and willing to discuss many aspects of their lives. The most interesting part of the class was the time they spent talking about prison and its impact on fathering. These young men spoke passionately about how going to prison had changed the relationships they had with their children and with their children's mother. As I attended more classes, I found myself spending a great deal of time thinking, talking, and reading about fathering and about incarceration. I discovered that few researchers had incorporated prison experience into their studies of fatherhood. My job at the CYA seemed to provide the perfect opportunity for research into the effects of incarceration and parole on young fathers.

The first project I envisioned focused on the establishment of legal paternity among parolees. After making this decision, I drove to Stockton to attend a parenting class. On discovering that the teacher was going to be late, I decided to test my research idea on some of the paroled fathers in the class. I hoped they would be enthusiastic and offer suggestions. To my disappointment, the men were not only unenthusiastic, they were downright hostile. They told me they were tired of judgmental researchers coming to ask them questions about topics they did not see as relevant to their lives. In a frustrated tone, one of them finally said that, if I wanted to do something useful, I should do a study about how difficult it is to be a paroled father. His comment, made in an offhand and half-joking manner, became the seed for this project. I ultimately focused on four questions involving the effect of incarceration and parole on young men's relationships with their children.

Fathering from Prison

Miguel was one of the young fathers I met during the course of this project. The first time I spoke with him he had just been paroled after spending two years in prison. A Latino father of one child, Miguel was fifteen years old the first time he was arrested. At the time of his arrest, his daughter Michelle was three months old. For the first half of his two-year sentence Miguel did not see Michelle because her maternal grandfather refused to let her come to prison. After Miguel pleaded with him, he relented and Michelle's mother brought her to visit once a month. The second time I met with Miguel, he had been rearrested and was serving his time at an outdoor camp several hours from his home. He had not seen his daughter for the five months he had been there. During our interview, Miguel spoke with great animation about his daughter and about the relationship he wanted to build with her. As he talked, however, he returned repeatedly to a discussion of how hard it was to maintain a relationship from prison.

Miguel was able to identity many of the ways in which the structure of the prison constrained his ability to be involved with his child. In chapter 2, I draw from my discussion with Miguel, as well as with other paroled fathers, to explore how the organization and the policies of the prison construct particular kinds of relationships between inmate fathers and their children. Research on the effects of adult prison policy suggest that the structure of the prison can shape inmates' personalities, relationships, and attitudes (Goffman 1961; Hairston 1995; McDermott and King 1992). In my analysis of the juvenile prison, I focus on the ways in which the gendered nature of the institution, its patriarchal/punitive structure, and its high-stress environment affect young fathers. I describe the involvement imprisoned fathers have with their children and explore some of the factors that encourage or discourage this involvement. These factors involve prison rules as well as the men's feelings about incarceration and about the relationships with their children's caretakers.

Young Fathers as Parolees

Miguel, like most incarcerated fathers, will eventually be released to parole and will be allowed, for a second time, to return home to his daughter. We know very little about the lives, attitudes, and experiences of young paroled fathers like Miguel. The few studies that have been done involve only adult, not juvenile, offenders and their children and focus primarily on the period of incarceration rather than on what happens once the fathers leave prison (Hale 1988). As a result, paroled men have been a largely unacknowledged segment of the young father population.

Part of the reason we have failed to pay attention to young paroled fathers is that research interest in the more general topic of young fatherhood is of fairly recent date. In the late 1960s, journalists and scholars began to discuss teenage pregnancy as a new social problem (Furstenberg, Brooks-Gunn, and Morgan 1987). This concern was fueled by a dramatic increase in the welfare rolls and by the rising number of out-of-wedlock births and single-parent families. An unfortunate limitation of the interest in teenage pregnancy was that it focused almost exclusively on teenage females. As a result, most research and intervention efforts were directed only toward girls and their children (Lerman and Ooms 1993). It was not until the 1980s that we began to see a growing interest in the role of fathers in teenage pregnancy.

Later in this chapter and in chapter 3, I look at patterns of fathering behaviors and attitudes among parolees. Some of the questions explored include: What are the characteristics of young paroled fathers? What does fatherhood mean to them? What fatherhood responsibilities do they fulfill? I address these questions with information about the paroled fathers' families of origin, criminal histories, current living arrangements, and children. In terms of information about father involvement, I focus on four specific indicators: paternity establishment, child support, visitation, and in-kind support. I chose these four areas because they are both formal and informal, economic and noneconomic. In addition, data already existed about these aspects of fatherhood, making it possible to draw comparisons between my subjects and those from other studies of young, poor fathers.

Complementing the discussion of paroled fathers' involvement with their children, chapter 4 presents information about the men's relationships with their families, their friends, and their children's mother and her family. Learning about the dynamics of these relationships is important because fathers do not interact with their children in a vacuum. A complex group of people potentially mediate, direct, discourage, or support the relationships between fathers and their children. Researchers have shown that the type and quality of relationship a man has with such people helps to determine his level of involvement with his children (Daly 1993; Danziger 1987; Furstenberg 1995; Seltzer and Brandreth 1994).

One of the unique features of this study is that the paroled fathers with whom I worked came from particularly diverse racial and ethnic backgrounds. This made it possible for me to explore differences between whites, blacks, and Latinos in terms of their levels and types of involvement with children. It also allowed for an examination of the ways in which men's relationships with their families, friends, and children's mothers are shaped by their race/ethnicity. To date, researchers have devoted little effort to studying young fathers who are not white or black. Zayas, Schinke, and Casareno (1987) point out that the lack of data on Latino fathers is particularly striking, since Latino adolescents are the fastest growing minority age group in the United States. Qualitative research suggests that there may be unique patterns of young fathering behavior among Latinos. For example, Mercer Sullivan (1993) did ethnographic work in a low-income Puerto Rican neighborhood and in a predominantly black neighborhood in New York and compared various aspects of fathering in the two neighborhoods. He found differences in marriage, in coresidence, and in employment patterns in the neighborhoods. He also found different patterns of support between the two groups. His findings suggest that intriguing information can be gained through inclusion of Latinos in our study of fatherhood.

Effect of the Prison on Later Father Involvement

Although Miguel was only on parole a few months before he was rearrested, he was out of prison long enough to recognize that his relationship with Michelle and her mother had changed substantially while he was gone. The literature on adult prisoners supports the idea that a father's absence due to incarceration can have devastating consequences for his long-term relationship with his children (McDermott and King 1992). Chapters 3 and 4 of this book explore incarceration's short-term and long-term effects on young paroled fathers' relationships with their children. The specific questions addressed include: How does prison time directly shape a parolee's relationship with his children? How does prison have indirect effects through changes in a man's relationships with his family, friends, and children's mother?

This investigation of the impact of prison on later life events and relationships adds to our understanding of the life course. Life course theory focuses on the progression of people's lives, paying particular attention to how personal biography and prevailing social norms interact to affect the timing and experience of such life transitions as marriage, divorce, and childbearing (Elder and O'Rand 1995). Life course researchers are also concerned with the results of life transitions and with their influence on the future of an individual. Any life transition profoundly affects other areas of a person's life. For example, getting married can have long-term repercussions on a person's career, lifestyle, education, and childbearing decisions. Much of the research done by life course researchers incorporates the idea of a "normative life course" in which particular transitions are presumed to precede others (Rindfuss, Swicegood, and Rosenfeld 1987). This normative life course assumes that people first finish school, then find employment, marry, and have children.

Young paroled fathers are an important group to investigate because they are in clear violation of the normative life course. In addition, time spent in prison is a potentially life-altering transition not taken into account by the normative life course perspective. While sociologists have studied the effects of an early transition to parenthood (for a review of the literature, see Furstenberg, Brooks-Gunn, and Morgan 1987), there has been little research on the transition into or out of prison. This kind of research is particularly consequential given evidence suggesting that a parolee's ability to develop and maintain strong social bonds may be linked to lower rates of recidivism. In a reanalysis of longitudinal data collected during the 1940s, Sampson and Laub (1993) found that juvenile delinquents who found good jobs, exciting educational opportunities, or stable marriages were sometimes able to move away from criminal behavior. If their conclusions are correct, it is extremely important that we increase our understanding of the impact of prison on these types of social bonds. In chapters 3 and 4, I discuss the links between education, employment, relationships, and prison for young paroled fathers.

Resolving Policy Contradictions

One of the promises I made to Miguel and to other paroled fathers I met over the course of this project is that I would use their words, thoughts, and experiences to craft policy suggestions. Many of the men hoped that their stories, once told, would help other incarcerated and paroled fathers. I fulfill my promise in the last chapter with an exploration of current juvenile justice policy and suggestions for the future. The goals of these suggested policy proposals are twofold: first, to encourage the development of healthy non-violent relationships between incarcerated and paroled men and their children; second, to mitigate the violence done to families and communities by the crimes and incarceration of young fathers.

Methods

The research for this project was conducted in four phases, each employing a different methodology. The idea was to make the study cumulative with each phase building on the preceding one and each intended to provide a different perspective on the lives and attitudes of young paroled fathers.

Observation in Parenting Classes

As part of my CYA job, I attended classes at four parole offices in Northern California. These classes were part of an ongoing pilot project by the CYA to provide parental education and support ser-vices to parolees. Class topics included child development, child rearing, discipline, and legal issues associated with fatherhood. The curriculum also contained sections designed specifically for the pa-rolee population. For instance, one session of the class was de-voted to a discussion of the transition from prison back into the lives of the young men's children. The Youth Authority encour-aged teachers to use the standardized curriculum but, at the same time, to plan their classes around the specific needs and concerns of the class participants.

Based on a set of criteria provided by the Youth Authority, pa-role agents selected fifteen to twenty young men to attend each twelve-week parenting class. The agents were instructed to give priority to biological fathers or to young men whose wives or girlfriends were pregnant. They were also allowed to admit young men who served in a father-figure capacity. For example, parolees who were primary caretakers for their younger siblings or for their girlfriend's children were qualified to attend. Once a man was selected by his agent, he was required to attend the class sessions. In reality, however, some of the men found excuses to avoid the classes, or they were rearrested and could not attend. As a result, the classes averaged about ten participants.

Between January and August 1996, I participated in approximately forty parenting class sessions. Although I was attending classes prior to these dates, it was not until January that I began to take systematic field notes. At the beginning of each new round of classes, I spent time talking to the parolees, telling them who I was and why I was there. I explained that I had been hired by the CYA to find ways to improve their classes. In addition, I told them that I was working on my own project about incarcerated and paroled fatherhood. Explaining my presence was necessary from an ethical standpoint, but it was also important because I was an obvious presence in the classes, different in gender, class, age, and race/ethnicity from the majority of the participants. Perhaps because of these differences, many of the men were initially suspicious of me. As the weeks passed, and the parolees watched me participate in class activities, they began to be more open. Some were interested in the fact that I was a student at the university and wanted to hear what it was like or how they could become students there. Many were fascinated by my project and wanted to talk about it. There were numerous occasions when parolees approached me before or after class sessions and volunteered stories about their own experiences.

The parenting classes I attended differed greatly by both site and individual session. In certain classes, parolees were extremely interested in the material, and the instructors were interrupted by frequent questions and comments. In these classes, the participants would often bring in questions about their own children to discuss with the teacher and with the other parolees in the class. Sometimes the conversation became so animated and loud that the parole office staff would come in to check on the situation. In contrast, the parolees in other classes were less talkative and the teacher spent more time lecturing.

My attendance at the parenting classes was a unique opportunity to learn about the concerns, problems, and fathering experiences of young parolees. Because most teachers made an effort to focus the classes on topics the young men requested, I was able to listen as the men discussed the issues they saw as most important in their lives. For example, in one class we talked about a man's fear that his neighbor was molesting his daughter. In another class we talked about problems several young men were having negotiating times to visit their nonresident children. The frequent group discussions, as well as the less-structured interaction of the men in the class, revealed much about their beliefs and feelings regarding fatherhood. The fact that classes were taught by community educators, not by CYA staff, gave them an informality that minimized pressure to please the teacher.

The parenting classes cannot be used as a direct source for making inferences about the entire population of young paroled fathers. My observations indicated that there was some bias in class selection because parole agents enrolled fathers who were having special problems with their children or, conversely, who were exceptionally involved with their kids. In addition, a few of the participants did not have children at all. In this book, I use examples from parenting classes when they are useful for illustrating some of the issues raised by the surveys and the in-depth interviews.

Survey

Based on eight months of observation in parenting classes, I constructed a survey to be administered to all paroled fathers in Northern California. The survey was designed to cover each man's current fathering practices, his experience as an incarcerated father, and his transition home to his children. For this reason, the questionnaire had to be fairly long (about 45 minutes to complete). To keep it a reasonable length, I asked each man to answer the questions in terms of his oldest child only. This decision was made because it increased the likelihood that a man had been incarcerated since the birth of that child.

After constructing the survey instrument, I conducted three phases of pretesting. This process proved invaluable. I found that my original questionnaire was sometimes unable to capture the men's experiences. A particularly memorable example of a problem in the original questionnaire involved two items that asked about residents in the household: one asked about adults, the other about children. To my surprise, these questions caused major confusion; the men kept asking me to define an adult and a child. I finally told them that an adult was over the age of eighteen. As a result of this definition, many were forced to categorize their underage wives and girlfriends as children. My assumptions about a normative life course resulted in these parolees feeling a great deal of embarrassment and discomfort. Ultimately I created just one item asking about the number of people in the household.

The final version of the questionnaire was ready in October 1996. At this time, I identified potential respondents from the seven parole offices in the Northern California region. These offices included Oakland, Stockton, Sacramento, Chico, San Jose, Fresno, and Bakersfield. As a California Youth Authority employee, it was easy for me to obtain a list of all the young men on parole in these offices. Unfortunately, no such list existed for paroled fathers. In order to overcome this problem, I used three complementary methods to identify the men on parole who had children. First, I asked all parole agents in Northern California to supply a list of the fathers in their caseloads. Parole agents, as part of their job, spend time out in the community with the young men and with their families and girlfriends. For this reason they are in a unique position to identify fathers, especially if a young man has fathered a child while on parole. The agents, however, may be less aware of children fathered before a young man's incarceration. To solve this problem, I obtained CYA records of intake interviews conducted when the men were first admitted to the system. In these interviews they were asked how many children they had. By combining parole agent lists and CYA intake records, I was able to identify fathers who had their children before they went to prison as well as those who had them afterward. Over the course of the year, I requested several updated lists from both sources in order to identify any new fathers who were being paroled. Using these sources I ultimately identified about 380 fathers.

I believe that the records from the parole agents and the Youth Authority provided a fairly complete list of parolees willing to identify themselves as fathers. Missing, however, were those unwilling to divulge their fatherhood status. Such men are sometimes afraid to admit paternity because they fear being reported to child support authorities; others simply do not want to hear a lecture about their responsibilities as fathers. To locate these men, I spent time in parole office waiting rooms talking with parolees. Most parolees are required to report to their agents at least once a month, so I was able to explain the study to a large number of young men. I assured all of them that this was a university, not a Youth Authority, study and that it was completely confidential. In this way I added twenty young fathers who were not on any list.

Using the three methods of identifying fathers, I created a list of 400 parolee fathers in Northern California. This list included men who had become fathers prior to their incarceration as well as those who had become fathers since being released. I believe that the list was fairly representative of the population of paroled fathers during the period of the study. It should be noted, however, that it was not necessarily representative of the population of incarcerated fathers. The two groups obviously have considerable overlap, but the paroled population excludes some of the more serious offenders who do not qualify for parole. Some of these offenders may never be released from prison, and those who are will be placed on adult parole, not on Youth Authority parole.

After compiling the list of paroled fathers, I began to set up appointments to administer the questionnaire. In the majority of cases I asked each father's parole agent to call and explain the study to him. In this way, the parolees were assured that the study was legitimate. I insisted that the agents stress the voluntary and confidential nature of the questionnaire. All potential respondents were also told that the project was being done by a researcher from the University of California and had nothing to do with the Youth Authority. Sometimes, when an agent was busy or unavailable, I or another interviewer contacted the young men. The process of contacting the men took twelve months, from October 1996 to October 1997.

Administering the questionnaire proved to be the most difficult stage of the research. Most of the young men had complicated schedules and multiple obligations. Many were employed far from their homes or were working at more than one job and could meet us for interviews only at very odd hours. In addition, a large number of young men either forgot our interview or did not make it at the scheduled time because they decided to do another activity instead. More often than not, the men were late for their interviews.

Many did not come at all, and as a result I had to reschedule a substantial percentage of the interviews, often numerous times. This was time-consuming and frustrating, especially when my interviewers and I had traveled many hours to meet with just one or a few parolees. I remember a particularly difficult day, during which we made the two-hour drive from Sacramento to San Jose, and none of the four scheduled interviewees appeared.

Of the 400 young men identified as fathers, I ultimately contacted 275; of these, 258 were interviewed. I was unable to contact 125 men, about half of whom were absent without leave (AWOL) and could not be located by the parole office. Almost as many had been returned to prison before I could interview them. Because parolees must report to their agents on a regular basis, it was fairly easy to locate all those men who were not AWOL. In a few cases, however, I had no success in finding the young men. This was a particular problem when agents were unavailable to help. At one office I encountered a "vacant caseload" problem—the agent had quit and a replacement had not yet been chosen. Young men from this caseload were difficult to contact because we were unsure who was a father. In addition, no one had updated their address/phone records in months, and many were living in new residences.

There were seventeen young men whom I contacted but who did not participate in the study: five refused; the other twelve agreed to be interviewed, but there were logistical problems that I simply could not overcome. The fact that only five men refused to participate is fairly remarkable. There are two reasons that help to explain this low refusal rate. First, after extensive discussion with Youth Authority staff, I decided to offer ten dollars in compensation to all the respondents. This offer encouraged the men to participate, and it also made the statement that their time was valuable. As parolees, these young men were compelled to attend many programs (victim awareness, drug treatment, parenting training, etc.). I wanted them to know that this project was different and that I appreciated the effort they were making. A second reason for the project's low refusal rate was that I made every effort to accommodate the needs of the young men. I generally tried to administer the surveys in parole offices, but when a parolee lived far from the office or did not have a ride, I would arrange to meet him in a public place near his home. For the men who lived in extremely rural areas, I arranged to interview them in their homes. My willingness to provide rides, bus money, and an occasional soda on a hot day further helped to encourage participation.

This project's 64 percent response rate does raise some concerns about sampling bias. As described, the vast majority of the men we failed to interview were either AWOL or had been sent back to prison before we could interview them. For this reason, the survey sample may underrepresent the more delinquent fathers on parole at the time. I believe that the fact that I was in the field for a full year, however, helped to minimize this problem. I was in frequent contact with agents and was able to identify and interview many fathers who had just been released from prison. Many of these men later disappeared or were sent back to prison soon after our interview.

All of the interviews were conducted in English. While a large number of the Latino respondents spoke Spanish as their first language, all were proficient enough in English to be able to complete the questionnaires. I suspect that we did not have language problems because most of the young men had grown up in the United States. Of those who had not, the time they spent in prison probably helped to make them fluent in English. The only time that English was an issue was in contacting the parolees to set up interviews. Many of their parents and grandparents spoke only Spanish. Fortunately, four of my interviewers and I all spoke fluent

Spanish, enabling us to communicate with these families and to enlist their help in setting up interviews.

As with most fatherhood research, this survey faced the potential problem of response bias. Response bias occurs when a respondent is less concerned about providing accurate answers than he is in maintaining a socially desirable image to the researcher. Research shows that men's accounts of their participation in child rearing often do not match official records or accounts given by the mothers of the children (Lareau 2000; Lerman 1993). Mothers, for example, tend to report that fathers pay less child support and spend less time with children than the fathers themselves report (Seltzer and Brandreth 1994). This study was designed to minimize such bias. First, I designed the survey to focus on the interaction of incarceration and fathering, rather than on fathering per se. Respondents were told that, while the project was about the fathering attitudes and behaviors of parolees, I was particularly interested in how incarceration affects fathering. In this way, respondents were less susceptible to social-desirability pressures because they believed that it was the prison system, more than their own fathering, that was being scrutinized.

The second way I minimized bias was through my choice of interviewers for the survey. I hired young female black, Latina, and white interviewers, and matched their race/ethnicity with that of the respondent. Research suggests that matching the race of interviewers and respondents makes for more honest survey responses (Schuman and Kalton 1985). In this project, I was able to match the race/ethnicity of the interviewer to that of the respondent in 80 percent of the cases. I did a number of analyses to check whether the 20 percent of cases that were not matched on race/ethnicity yielded significantly different responses from those that were matched. These analyses suggested that the responses from the two groups were essentially the same. While I was pleased to find no evidence of bias, I did momentarily mourn the many hours that had gone into the matching process.

When I designed the survey, I planned to hire male interviewers in order to match respondent/interviewer gender as well as race, but the CYA staff urged me to reconsider this decision. They uniformly agreed that women elicit more honest responses from this population than do men. From working with parolees in many parenting classes, I came to agree strongly with this assessment. The fact that the men are more comfortable discussing parenting issues with a woman may be because they are less accustomed to talking about intimate topics with other men. Furthermore, the pressure for parolees to uphold male group norms is not as strong with a female interviewer as with a man. Ultimately, I decided to hire seven female interviewers from local colleges and universities and to conduct surveys myself.

In addition to the focus of the survey and the choice of interviewers, I minimized bias by rigorous pretesting and by my attendance in the twelve-week parenting classes. These classes provided me with the opportunity to get to know the parolee population outside the survey situation and to ensure that the survey questionnaire I constructed was culturally and linguistically relevant to the parolees. Pretesting helped meet these same goals. I went over the first draft of the survey with a group of three parolees, and we talked about each question's wording, response categories, and relevance. After substantially reworking the survey, I pretested it with twenty-five fathers at a parole office in Southern California. This pretest provided invaluable information for a further refining of the survey questions. As a final test, I took the revised survey to another group of three parolees to finalize question wording and order.

The final copy of the survey contained a number of retrospective questions that can introduce reliability problems. People's ability to remember past events diminishes in accuracy and detail over time. One of the reasons for this is that people may reorganize memories of past events to be compatible with their present lives. Such reliability problems are minimized in this study because I asked about events that happened recently and were important in respondents' lives. Research indicates that respondents recall recent events better than distant events and that reliability increases with the salience of the questions (Fowler 1995). From observations and interviews with the young men, I found that fatherhood and incarceration issues were of such importance to them that few had difficulty remembering details about subjects such as the birth of their child, visits in prison, or breakups with their girlfriend. Their memory was helped by the fact that most had been out of prison for less than a year.

In-Depth Interviews

After doing preliminary analysis of the survey data, I constructed an in-depth interview schedule. The first section contained general questions about fathering and incarceration. Subsequent sections asked about the young men's experiences with being fathers in prison, their transition home to their children, and their attitudes about being fathers and about fatherhood in general. I decided to conduct twenty in-depth interviews. To select candidates from the original group of 258 survey respondents, I used a purposive sampling strategy. I began by excluding from consideration two groups of young men. First, I excluded the thirteen young men who told us, at the time of the survey, that they were not interested in doing another interview. Then I disqualified young men who had not been incarcerated for any period of time since the birth of their oldest child. This decision was consistent with the project's focus on the intersection of fathering and incarceration and excluded just under 23 percent of the remaining survey respondents.

From the remaining 183 young men, the computer randomly selected 20. I then checked to make sure that this group was representative of all survey respondents. I made some minor adjustments to ensure that it was geographically representative and that it contained a representative number of involved and noninvolved fathers. I adjusted the group by adding randomly selected parolees from the underrepresented groups. Race/ethnicity was the only variable that was not selected to be closely matched to the population. I made the decision to include at least five men from each of the three major racial/ethnic groups (white, Latino, black) so that I could maximize the racial/ethnic variation. To this end, I chose an in-depth interview sample that included five white respondents, seven blacks, and eight Latinos.

The in-depth interview sample was fairly representative of the survey respondents in terms of marital status, employment, father involvement, and age. I also retained three young men who were not representative of the majority of respondents but had attributes that added important diversity to this small sample. One of these young men had sole custody of his daughter, one had three children by three women, and one had never seen his child and refused to have any contact with him. By allowing a few unrepresentative cases to stay in the sample, I was able to get a sense of the entire range of young paroled fathers.

All twenty of the men I contacted agreed to be reinterviewed. The in-depth interviews were conducted in a number of locations, depending on where the young men lived and what was most convenient for them. Over a third of the interviews were conducted in the men's homes or in a public place, such as a library. When an interview took place in a home, I always made sure that other people were there but that we were in a private space. A third of the interviews were conducted at parole offices. Because four of the men I had selected had been reincarcerated, their interviews took place in a separate area at the specific institution. Two of the four were housed at CYA facilities, and two had been placed under the supervision of the California Department of Corrections. I personally conducted all of the in-depth interviews, and all interviews were tape-recorded and transcribed directly.

Participant Observation at Institutional Visiting Hours

In the fall of 1998 I went to three California Youth Authority prisons to observe the conditions under which inmates receive visits from children. This observation augmented the descriptions given me by respondents in the survey and in-depth interviews, and it provided a way to check the accuracy of their reports. I also talked with the prison staff about their perspectives on the value and effects of allowing children to visit inmates.

I started at the Northern Reception Center and Clinic (NRCC) because all the fathers in my survey had spent some time there. NRCC provides interim housing for young people who have just entered the system or who are being temporarily detained on parole violations. These youths generally do not stay more than a few months before being released or going on to regular placements. There are, however, a few with special needs who serve their full sentence at NRCC.

I also visited two regular CYA institutions, Chaderjian Prison and DeWitt Nelson, both in Stockton. I chose these institutions because they house a large number of wards (about seven hundred inmates at one, and close to a thousand at the other) and both are intended for older wards (over the age of eighteen). I focused on this population because older wards tend to have more children than do younger, and visiting these institutions maximized my chances of witnessing father/child contact. I also chose the institutions because over 40 percent of my respondents had spent time in one or both of these institutions. It was important that I visit more than one institution because the visiting conditions vary somewhat from institution to institution. This variation is explained in part by the fact that different levels of offenders are grouped at different institutions, and the security requirements are tailored accordingly. To get a sense of this range, I chose to visit one institution that houses the most serious offenders and a second that houses less serious offenders.

I spent at least two hours at each prison, talking with the staff and observing the visiting. I explained to the staff why I was there, and all of them welcomed questions about how the institutions operate. During these sessions I stayed to the side of the visiting area and tried to be as unobtrusive as possible. A few of the inmates and their families greeted me. But, other than that, no one seemed to notice my presence. There was no indication that I affected the normal operation of visiting hours in any way. My ability to fit in was helped by the fact that I wore a badge and probably appeared to be a CYA staff member.

Paroled Fathers: Lives and Experiences

The paroled fathers who participated in the surveys and in-depth interviews lived in towns and cities scattered all over Northern California. In total, the interviewers and I conducted surveys with young men in 70 cities with populations ranging from less than 1,000 to more than 780,000. About half of the fathers lived in the large urban centers (Sacramento, Fresno, Oakland, and San Jose). Because the interviewers and I met many of the men at or near their homes, we were able to observe the conditions in their neighborhoods. Most of the urban men came from areas characterized by concentrated poverty—neighborhoods that would be classified as "inner city" or "underclass." At the other end of the spectrum, about 20 percent of paroled fathers lived in rural areas or relatively small towns (defined as a population under 50,000). Some of the rural fathers lived many miles from their nearest neighbor, and others lived in small migrant farmworker communities scattered throughout the Central Valley.

The households in which the parolees lived tended to be fairly large (4.5 people on average). About 43 percent of the men lived with one or both of their parents, and 39 percent lived with their wives or girlfriends. The rest lived with grandparents, with friends, or alone. About 30 percent lived in households that included their oldest children. It should be noted, however, that this figure is a one-day average. The fathers tended to have a great deal of mobility into and out of the households of their children. Of men who were not living with their children at the time of the survey, 56 percent had lived with them at least once in the past, usually for a short period. The average length of time they lived with their children was ten weeks.

The fact that so many of the fathers lived with parents or grandparents made it difficult to calculate their household income accurately. This became clear when I pretested the survey instrument and only a small number of the respondents were able to estimate their parents' income. As a proxy for household income, I asked the men about household welfare receipt and employment. Thirty-six percent of the fathers reported that they lived in a household in which someone received Aid to Families with Dependent Children (AFDC). This was considerably higher than the 5 percent of families nationwide and the 7.5 percent of Californians who received AFDC (DiNitto 1995, 187). In terms of employment, 40 percent of the parolees lived in a household in which there were no wage earners or in which they were the sole wage earner. These levels of welfare receipt and employment point to the fact that there is a much greater level of household poverty among paroled fathers than there is in the general population.

California is one of the most racially heterogeneous states in the nation. The paroled fathers were correspondingly diverse, although as a group they did not exactly reflect the racial composition of California. Because poor and minority men are overrepresented both in the correctional system and in the pool of young fathers, the percentage of paroled fathers who are Latino and black is greater than their representation in the state population. Table 1.1 shows the race/ethnicity of paroled fathers, that of all male parolees in Northern California, and that of the general population of young men in California. It should be noted that these racial/ethnic comparisons are approximations because I include a "multiracial" category for the paroled fathers.[2] Neither the Youth Authority nor

Table 1.1 Race/Ethnicity of Fathers, Ages 15-24, on Parole in the Northern Region of the California Youth Authority

Race/Ethnicity	Fathers on Parole (N=258)	All Male Parolees in Northern California, 1996 (N=2,808)	All California males, ages 15-24, 1996 (N=2,198,841)
White	33 (12.8%)	613 (21.8%)	45.1%
Black	71 (27.5%)	688 (24.5%)	8.3%
Latino	125 (48.4%)	1,180 (42.0%)	34.1%
Asian/Pacific Islander/ Native American	16 (6.2%)	309 (11.0%)	12.5%
Multiracial	13 (5.0%)	Not available	Not available

Father statistics are taken from author's survey data. Regional parolee statistics are taken from California Youth Authority, *Characteristics of CYA Population* (Sacramento: Research Division, Ward Information and Parole Research Bureau, 1996). California statistics are taken from the California Department of Finance, *1992–1996 Population: 1970–1996 Race/Ethnic Population Estimates by County with Age and Sex Detail* (Sacramento: Department of Finance, 1998).

the state of California compiles racial/ethnic statistics using this category.

The largest group of the paroled fathers (about 48 percent) were Latino. This is not surprising given the fact that 25 percent of California's population is Latino and poverty is disproportionately concentrated in Latino communities (DiNitto 1995). Although the label "Latino" usually refers to a diverse group of people of South American, Central American, Cuban, and Puerto Rican origin, over 90 percent of the Latino paroled fathers were of Mexican descent. This reflects the composition of California in which just under 80 percent of Latinos are of Mexican origin (U.S. Bureau of the Census 1992). About half of the Latino paroled fathers had parents who were born outside the United States, while the parents of the other half were born here. Following Latinos, the two largest groups of paroled fathers were blacks (28 percent) and whites. Whites represented 21 percent of the Youth Authority population, but they constituted only 13 percent of the fathers, perhaps because whites in the general population are somewhat less likely than Latinos or blacks to become fathers as teenagers (Lerman 1993).

Close to 70 percent of the paroled fathers had one child, 22 percent had two, and 8 percent had three or four. Over half of the parolees became fathers as teenagers. The youngest of the fathers was 12 when he had his first child, and the oldest was 24. The average age was 17.9 years. Since the average age of the paroled fathers was 20.7 years at the time of the survey, the average age of the children was about two and a half years. Table 1.2 shows the distribution of fathers' ages at the birth of the eldest child.

It is interesting to note that while research indicates that the majority of teen mothers are impregnated by adult men (Moore 1995), parolees tend to have children with women who are close in age. The median age of the mothers was seventeen years at the birth of the parolees' oldest child.

Table 1.2 Ages of Parolees in Northern California at Time of Eldest Child's Birth

Age When First Child Born	Fathers (N=250)	% of Sample
12–13	3	31.2
14–15	37	14.8
16–17	87	34.9
18–19	74	29.6
20–21	30	12.0
22–23	17	6.8
24	2	.8

All statistics taken from author's survey data. Age information was not obtained from 8 of the original 258 fathers on parole.

Only 3 percent of the children of parolees were conceived within a marriage. Most of the pregnancies of parolees' partners occurred within the context of a dating relationship. About 15 percent of the men had their oldest child as a result of a "one-night stand." Frank Furstenberg (1995) points out that romantic relationships between young parents tend to be transient and unstable. This is partly because adolescents do not have much experience with being in relationships, but it is also because many do not know each other well when the woman becomes pregnant. This description is most certainly apt for many of the parolees. The average couple had been dating for six months when the woman became pregnant. One-fourth had known each other two months or less when they learned of the pregnancy.

The primary reason that the parolees and their partners became pregnant so quickly after the start of the relationships is that few were using any type of birth control. Two-thirds of the survey respondents reported that they never used contraception with their partner, and another 22 percent said that they only used it "some of the time." About a quarter of the men said that they were not using birth control because they were actively trying to have a child; the rest of the pregnancies were unplanned.

When the young men learned about their partners' pregnancies, they experienced a wide range of emotions, but the overwhelming reaction was one of surprise. This is somewhat perplexing given that only a few had been using any type of birth control. The men reported, however, that they simply had not given much thought to the possibility that their partner might become pregnant. In one survey item I asked the parolees to rate on a scale from 0 to 5 how surprised they felt when they first heard that their partner was pregnant. Over 60 percent said 5. To say that the young men were surprised by the pregnancies of their partners is not, however, to say that they were unhappy about becoming fathers. Most reported that they were very happy when they found out their partners were pregnant. Close to 60 percent reported that, on a happiness scale of 0 to 5, they felt a 5 when they heard the news. The men also felt a great deal of pride. Again, close to 60 percent told me that they had felt "very proud" when they first knew they were going to be fathers. Corresponding to these positive feelings about fatherhood, most men did not consider abortion as an option. Three-quarters reported that they had not thought about abortion at all, and only 6 percent said they had seriously considered it.

Part of the way that the men expressed their happiness about the pregnancies of their partners was to participate in some way during the pregnancy. Over 80 percent provided food or money for their pregnant partner, and about the same number bought baby supplies in preparation for the child's arrival. About 75 percent accompanied the mother to one or more of her doctor's appointments, and over 20 percent attended childbirth classes with her. Few, how-

Table 1.3 Crimes Committed by Fathers Paroled in the Northern Region of the California Youth Authority

Crime	Fathers	All Male CYA Parolees in 1996
Crimes against property:		
auto theft	23 (10.5%)	264 (9.3%)
burglary	21 (9.5%)	439 (15.5%)
theft	15 (6.8%)	214 (7.6%)
Crimes against people		
drug sales/possession	19 (8.6%)	206 (7.3%)
robbery	37 (16.9%)	516 (18.3%)
assault	81 (36.8%)	836 (29.6%)
sex crimes (except rape)	6 (2.7%)	72 (2.5%)
kidnapping	2 (.9%)	17 (.6%)
rape	6 (2.7%)	50 (1.8%)
homicide	7 (3.2%)	71 (2.5%)
Other offenses	3 (1.4%)	126 (4.5%)
Total	220	2,825

Information was not available for 38 of the original 258 fathers on parole. Father statistics are taken from CYA intake records. Youth Authority statistics are taken from California Youth Authority, *Characteristics of CYA Population* (Sacramento: Research Division, Ward Information and Parole Research Bureau, 1996).

ever, decided that marriage was an appropriate response to the pregnancy. Only 4 percent of the men married the mothers of their child after the conception or birth.

Turning to the paroled fathers' criminal histories, table 1.3 shows the crimes committed. It should be noted that these figures reflect committing offenses, not complete criminal histories. Because the Youth Authority houses the most serious offenders in California, most of the paroled fathers had extensive criminal histories. The committing offense is the crime that caused the men to be sent to the CYA for the first time. When a person committed multiple crimes simultaneously, the most serious is generally listed as the committing offense. This method of categorizing crime masks secondary crimes such as drug use, and it also hides subsequent criminal convictions.

It is useful to clarify several of the terms in table 1.3. Under the heading "Crimes against Property," burglary means illegally entering a structure for the purpose of committing a felony or theft. Theft means taking someone else's property. Under "Crimes against People," robbery means taking the property of another using violence or intimidation. Sex crimes primarily include public exposure and child molestation. From the data presented in table 1.3, it appears that the paroled fathers' criminal histories are fairly similar to those of the parolee population in general. Burglary offenses are slightly underrepresented in the father group, and assault is overrepresented.

The paroled fathers had been sent to CYA facilities between one and five times. Most (71 percent) had been in once, 19 percent twice, and 7 percent had been in three times. These figures reflect only the number of times men had been sentenced to a CYA facility; they do not include temporary detainment for parole violations, nor do they reflect commitments to county or local juvenile detention facilities. The paroled fathers had served between 2 and 96 months in CYA institutions. The average total for time served was 30.4 months.

Of the men who participated in the survey, 185 (74 percent) had spent time in prison since the birth of their child. The children of the remaining 26 percent were born after the men's release.

2

Fathering from Behind Bars

All correctional facilities in the United States have strict rules governing the contact that inmates have with the outside world. These limitations are intended as a security measure and as part of an inmate's punishment. Interestingly, the rules that govern the outside contact of juvenile inmates are even more restrictive than the policies in adult correctional facilities (Bortner and Williams 1997). These institutional rules obviously have profound implications for the relationships that incarcerated fathers are able to build or maintain with their children.

Juvenile facilities in the United States generally allow incarcerated fathers to have three kinds of contact with their children—letters, telephone calls, and visitation. At the California Youth Authority, telephone policy varies by institution and is tied to inmate conduct in the prison. Most inmates are restricted from receiving incoming calls but are allowed to make at least one collect call a week. At some institutions, inmates who exhibit good behavior are allowed to make several telephone calls in any given week. The rules at the CYA are fairly similar to those found in other juvenile institutions nationally. A report published by the National Office of Juvenile Justice and Delinquency Prevention notes that most juveniles in correctional facilities can place a limited number of telephone calls per week. Unlike the inmates at the CYA, about 55 percent of juvenile inmates nationally can also receive a limited number of incoming calls (Parent et al. 1994). Letter writing policy at most institutions is more lenient than the telephone policy. Inmates can generally send as many letters as they like, provided they have stamps and the prison staff approves the content of the letters.

Most incarcerated fathers take advantage of their ability to make calls and to write to children. In the survey, about 80 percent of the men said that while they were incarcerated they spoke with their children on the telephone. In addition, most men (over 85 percent) talked to their children's caretakers to find out how the children were doing. Just under 75 percent reported sending their child a letter, and about 70 percent received a picture their child had drawn. Not surprisingly, men with infants were less likely to have written to their children or received mail from them.

Of all the types of contact inmates can have with their children, visitation is the most obvious and direct. It is also the area in which correctional institutions exert the most control. From the beginning of a young man's stay at the CYA, policies limit his access to his child. New inmates are generally denied visiting privileges during their first few weeks at the institution. This policy is intended to be a security measure, but it also succeeds in separating inmates from their lives on the outside, including their children. Prisons are not the only institutions to engage in such practices. Erving Goffman, in his work examining life in a variety of institutions, points out that policies of this sort are common; they are a way of "ensuring a deep initial break with past roles and appreciation of role dispossession" (Goffman 1961, 114).

After the first few weeks in the institution, most CYA inmates are allowed to begin a normal visiting schedule. This means that they are allowed to receive up to four visitors for several hours every two weeks, or every week at a few institutions. Visitation with children actually occurs far less often. About 22 percent of the men reported that they saw their child weekly; another 17 percent reported seeing their child two or three times a month. A few (6 percent) visited with their child monthly. Another 22 percent saw their children infrequently, meaning that they saw their children only once or twice during their entire stay in the CYA. Just over 33 percent did not see their children at all. There were no significant differences between the racial and ethnic groups in the amount of reported visitation.

There are many reasons young incarcerated fathers fail to use all the time allowed to see their children. Setting aside reasons that originated before their incarceration, the men reported that three sets of institutional rules limited the number of times they saw their children—inmate placement policy, visiting-list restrictions, and entrance requirements.

Only One Girlfriend: Official Limits on Father/Child Contact

Youth Authority institutions and camps are scattered throughout the state of California, and inmates can be assigned to any of these facilities. Sometimes men are placed hundreds of miles from their home, and their families find it difficult, if not impossible, to visit. Even when inmates are placed closer to home, many families find it hard to visit because they do not have cars or gas money or they have to work on the designated visiting day. Juveniles nationally are confined an average of 58 miles from their homes (Parent et al. 1994).

Many of the paroled fathers talked about the serious problems their families had finding transportation to the institution. About a third reported that these transportation problems sometimes prevented them from seeing their child. One man told me that he was not able to see his son very much because his grandmother was the only person in his family with access to a vehicle. About a year into his two-year sentence, his grandmother died and the young man was not able to see his child until his release. While there are nonprofit groups that provide transportation to some of the institutions, the services are simply not sufficient to help all the families needing assistance.

Each inmate is allowed to submit a list of people they would like to be allowed to visit. Institutional staff then determine which of the people are eligible and establish the inmate's official "visiting list." People on the visiting list must be members of the inmate's immediate family—parents, siblings, grandparents, and biological children. At most institutions (although not at all), an inmate can also see his wife or girlfriend. These visiting-list rules were created to ensure institutional security and to prevent overcrowding at visiting hours. Their unintended result, however, is to keep some men from seeing their children.

A man who has children by several women can list only one in the "girlfriend" or "wife" category. Since mothers are the primary people bringing children to the institution, inmates must make a choice about which of their children they want to see. I asked one young man what he had done when faced with this choice. He told me that he chose the mother who was least angry with him. On the rare occasion that he was allowed to make changes to his list, he would switch the women. This strategy was obviously not ideal and ultimately managed to alienate both women. As a result, he ended up missing substantial periods in the lives of his children.

The "one girlfriend" rule is also a problem for men whose girlfriends are not the mothers of their children. In these cases men are forced to choose between their girlfriend and the mother of their child. Few can resist seeing their girlfriends, even when it means they cannot see their child. Some inmates solve "one girlfriend" dilemmas by arranging for their own mothers or another member of their family to bring the children, but this strategy is contingent on the willingness of the mother to send her child to the institution without her. Because relationships between incarcerated men and the mothers of their children are often extremely tenuous, some mothers are unwilling to allow their children to go to the institution with the inmate's family. Of the 125 men who received visits from their children in prison, 49 percent reported that their children's mother was the primary person to bring children, and about 38 percent reported that their own mothers brought the children most often.

Visitors can be denied entry to the institution for a variety of reasons. First, visitors must have proper identification with them, and girlfriends and wives under the age of eighteen must have a notarized letter from one of their parents giving them permission to visit. In addition, all visitors must meet the dress code. This code specifies that women are not allowed to be provocatively attired, and it specifically forbids tight clothing and short skirts. No visitors, male or female, are allowed to wear shorts or display gang symbols or colors. These rules are enforced by the staff. During one of my visits to the prison, I saw a man being asked to leave because he was wearing shorts. Visitors who are turned away are allowed to go back to their cars and change their clothes or, at certain facilities, they can go to a hospitality house to borrow clothes. If, for whatever reason, they cannot change clothes, they are simply asked to leave. Over 20 percent of the men who spent time in prison since the birth of their child reported that they had been denied at least one visit with their child because a member of their family was in violation of the dress code or other rules.

When families are turned away from institutions, children miss the opportunity to see their fathers. More serious, however, is the possibility that, fearing they again will not be allowed to enter, families become less willing to make the long trip to the institution. This fear is not unfounded, especially because there are days when no one is admitted to the institution. This is called "lockdown," and it occurs when there has been fighting, a riot, or the threat of a riot. Individuals, groups, or entire institutions can be put on "lockdown" and not allowed to receive visits. About 36 percent of survey respondents who had been to prison since the birth of their child reported that a lockdown had prevented at least one visit with their child. Usually when a lockdown occurs, inmates are able to call their families and tell them not to come, but sometimes the lockdown occurs the night before visiting day. In these cases families arrive at the institution and are denied entry. When asked if lockdown ever affected his visiting day, Miguel said:

> It happened to me twice. . . . The first time was because of something the hall did. . . . They just told us to call our parents and tell them they can't come. But some were already there. The second time was a group that I was hanging around with did something and they locked us down. . . . They didn't even tell us nothing about visiting. . . . I was out like maybe two weeks later. . . . I called my family and I asked them. Then my brother started yelling at me, "What did you do? . . . 'Cause we went over there and they wouldn't let us in."

Charles, a twenty-two-year-old who served three years on drug charges, talked about lockdown during his in-depth interview:

> Charles: During some of the visits . . . fights break out, and then it turns into a big riot, and then the visits are terminated. And then when they have like the riot in the institution, they take everybody's visits, you know. Then you just can't get a visit that weekend because north to south had a riot or something like that, and they just cut all the visits off.

A.N.: Did anybody ever come to see you and weren't able to get in?

Charles: The one visit, like the riot kicked off probably like a Saturday night, or a Friday night, and then they stopped all the visits. They came up because I wasn't able to notify them in time, because we was all in lockdown, so I wasn't able to use the phone or anything.

Families such as Charles's work hard to find transportation to the prison. When they are turned away, they may be discouraged from making a return visit.

All of these policies—inmate placement, visiting lists, and entrance requirements—have a reason for their existence. For example, inmates are placed in age-graded institutions for their own safety. Visitors are limited so that visiting hours do not become overcrowded. Only immediate family members are allowed in as part of the men's punishment and also as part of an effort to limit their contact with former gang associates. The fact of the matter is, however, that these rules also stand in the way of men's ability to build relationships with their children.

Nothing to Do: Children at Visiting Hours

Visiting hours are the primary way that men can build relationships with their children from prison; consequently, they are the focus of high expectations and excitement. Many of the inmates have not seen their children in months and eagerly anticipate their arrival. Alberto, a Latino father of a toddler, was back in the institution at the time of his interview. He told me:

It feels good, just to know that I'm getting a visit this Sunday—my mom's coming, my son's going to come—'cause I miss my son a whole lot and it's like—it feels different. I can't explain the feeling but it's like—it feels good 'cause you want to see him and it's been awhile and you finally see him—oh, that's my son, and you start telling your son how much you love him.

Jeremy, a father of two children, talked about the importance of visiting hours. He felt that they had allowed him to keep a connection with his youngest child:

> From the time she was born to when she was ten months . . . she come up there every week visiting me. So we'd talk and I seen her growing every week, you know. I didn't see her seven days a week, only once every week. So she knew me. . . . She knows me real good.

When I observed institutional visiting hours, I watched the obvious happiness with which many of the inmates greeted their children. It was clear that they were excited to see the children and to spend time with them. After the initial excitement wore off, however, visiting hours turned out to be a disappointment for many of the men. Often the structure of visiting hours interferes with positive father/child interaction.

At CYA facilities, visiting hours take place in two locations: a large room filled with tables, and an adjoining outdoor patio area. The outside areas have trees and picnic tables and, at some facilities, there are barbecues available. Eating is the central activity during visiting hours. At some institutions, families can bring food from the outside, and many arrive with bags of chicken or hamburgers. At other institutions, families are limited to purchasing food from the vending machines in the institution. When they are not eating, inmates and their visitors sit at the tables or walk around in the yard. On rainy days, everything must take place inside, and the visiting hours become quite loud and chaotic.

The Youth Authority strives to "normalize" visiting hours so that the facility feels friendly and not institutional. Prisons that allow barbecuing and outside food are especially good at creating a welcoming atmosphere. None of the efforts, however, can hide the extensive security precautions, the barbed wire, and the guards. As a result, older children are quite aware that they are in prison. For many inmates, their children's awareness causes them to feel shame and embarrassment during visiting hours. About half of the survey respondents who received visits from their children said that they had felt this way during their visits. Paul, a father of a two-year-old son, said:

> I felt ashamed because the first time he ever got to see me he saw me in jail. You know, my hopes and dreams when I was a little kid was to have my family. If I was to have a kid from anybody I wanted my kids and the mother of my kids to be together forever. You know, be like my mom and my dad wasn't. So I wanted to make my kids better than what I had. But it didn't turn out that way.

Tony, an eighteen-year-old who was back in prison at the time of his in-depth interview, talked about his embarrassment when his son became old enough to start asking him questions:

> Actually, the last time he came and saw me, it was two weeks ago. . . . The visit was almost going to end . . . and he's like, "Are you coming home with us?" And it shocked me. I just sat there for a moment, and I told him no. And he said, "Why?" I said, "They won't let me go yet." He said, "Well, make them let you go." I said, "No, I gotta stay here 'til it's time for me to go home." And he just came back to me, "Why?" I was shocked. A three-year-old baby. Where are these questions coming from? I was hurt. I felt low actually. I felt like I was the lowest man in the planet. . . . It wasn't so bad when he was too young, you know what I'm saying, to even remember this, but now he's starting to realize what's happening, where I'm at, why I'm here. You know, I did something wrong, so now I've got to stay here. I don't know if he realizes how long

it's going to be 'til he gets to see me again. It made me feel bad. It was like the lowest thing on this planet.

Sometimes young fathers were so ashamed of being seen by their children in prison that they chose to refuse visits altogether. Of the sixty men who did not see their children at all, about 20 percent told me that shame was one of the reasons, and about 10 percent said shame was the single most important reason. Miguel talked about his fears of letting his daughter see him in the institution:

> [I was afraid of] her looking at me different. Like, "My dad . . . what is my dad? Is he a gangster? A killer? What is he in here for? What did he do?" I don't want her to be afraid of me, basically what I'm saying. 'Cause basically, I mean, I've seen a lot of the public when they see us working out there [on work crews]. They're kind of scared of us, and I don't like that. I don't want them to be scared of me. I'm not going to do nothing to them. I don't want her to see that, too. I don't want her to be afraid of me just 'cause I'm incarcerated.

It appears that while men of all races and ethnicities experience shame about their incarceration, the level of shame varies somewhat by racial/ethnic group. Latinos, as a group, are slightly more likely than blacks or whites to report feeling ashamed of being seen in prison.[1] On closer examination, however, it becomes clear that degree of shame is more closely linked to generation in the United States. The level of reported shame of Latino respondents whose parents were born outside of the United States is higher than that of respondents whose parents were born here. While over 50 percent of the Latino respondents with foreign-born parents agreed that they felt shame about their children seeing them in prison, only 30 percent of the rest of the sample agreed. About 38 percent of Latinos with native-born parents reported feeling shame. It appears that shame about incarceration decreases as a family's time in the

United States increases. This finding corresponds with the work of other researchers who have found that first- and second-generation Latinos have attitudes and behaviors that are significantly different from later generations (Suarez-Orozco and Suarez-Orozco 1995).

Shame causes visiting hours to be awkward and embarrassing for some men. Further increasing this awkwardness is the fact that there are few opportunities for "normal" interaction between fathers and their children. Outside prison, men generally relate to children through play or other social activities (Bailey 1994). This simply is not possible in the institution because, at most facilities, there are no toys. This makes it difficult to interact with children or to keep them entertained. About 20 percent of the survey respondents said that their children sometimes did not like coming to visit at the institution because "there was nothing for them to do there." A staff member at one of the institutions told me that they do allow families to bring in a limited number of toys, but none of the families I saw had any. Several staff members told me that the limitations on toys were a necessary security measure because drugs could easily be placed inside.

Not having toys or games is a particular problem for the juvenile-inmate population because so few have experience with their children. Most have been in prison throughout their children's lives, and even those who were involved with them before they were incarcerated must adjust to each new developmental stage. Toys or games would provide some way for men to relate to their children. As it stands, visiting hours can be extremely tense and uncomfortable. I watched one young child, clearly bored, who kept wandering away from the table where her parents were visiting. The inmate kept ordering her back, and both he and the child ended up looking frustrated and exhausted. Marco, a nineteen-year-old Latino father from a small town in the Central Valley, talked about visiting with his daughter while he was incarcerated:

You don't pay attention to your kid when they come visit you there. Some people do, but other times, I noticed I wasn't. I mean, I was, but then I wasn't. My mind was other places, my eyeballs and everything. You're always looking around over here and over there, and seeing people you know and whoop-de-whoop, and the kids are just there running around. You've got to chase 'em. There ain't nowhere for them to play or nothing. You know, you miss 'em and everything. You hug 'em. They might sit on your lap and everything. But after fifteen or twenty minutes any kid would get bored just seeing a bunch of people, a bunch of chairs and tables. What's the use of them being there?

Tony served an eleven-month sentence and was back in prison at the time of his in-depth interview. He talked about some of the problems he was having during visiting hours, including difficulty keeping his child entertained.

Yeah, but I found a solution. Candy. He used to like coming to see me at YA because he got more junk food on visiting days than you got throughout the week. Junk food, junk food. We'd play, wrestle a little bit. I'd tire him out, go to sleep. . . . It's hard because you're thinking about the kid. You want to be playful, but then you're trying to focus on a serious conversation. Once you get into the serious conversation, the kid decides you don't want to play no more, they want to be obnoxious. They want to make noise and run all around. It do get kind of complicated.

From my observations and the reports from the young men, it appears that eating is the primary activity the fathers engage in with their children. Once the food is gone, many of the fathers simply hand the children over to the mothers.

A final aspect of visiting hours that interferes with "normal" interaction between fathers and their children is that men usually receive several visitors at once. Visiting hours occur only once a week or once every other week, and inmates often want to see several members of their family as well as their girlfriend. At the institution, I noticed many of the young men tried to engage in serious conversations with their adult visitors, but they were so distracted by their children that they could not communicate well. Visiting children have nothing to do at prison, and so they demand almost constant attention. The young men, torn between their desire to talk with their girlfriends or family members and their desire to pay attention to their children, are not able to do a very good job of either.

Fathers' Responses to the Prison Environment

The general structure of the institution encourages fathers to develop particular attitudes and coping mechanisms that affect the relationships they have with their children. My interactions with the paroled fathers suggest that there are few differences, other than levels of reported shame, between black, white, and Latino fathers in their responses to the prison environment. This is somewhat surprising given studies documenting racial variations. For example, Leo Carroll's 1974 work on race relations inside a maximum security prison suggested that blacks and whites enter prison with different orientations. The blacks in his study tended to be more politicized and less willing to submit to the system. Whites, on the other hand, were less likely to feel that an injustice had been done them and were more submissive to prison rules and policies. Bartollas, Miller, and Dinitz's work (1976) with juvenile inmates in Ohio showed that blacks and whites had different codes of conduct and held to these codes with different levels of intensity. Similarly, Toch (1992) found that black and white inmates exhibited different "focal concerns," with blacks focusing most on their desire for freedom and whites on their need for social support. It is not clear why the racial/ethnic differences identified in these previous studies did not appear among the paroled fathers in my study.

The explanation may have to do with the different time periods in which the studies were conducted, the different populations, or the types of questions that were asked.

In the following sections, I describe common reactions of the men in this study to the prison environment.

Hard Timing

Juvenile correctional facilities across the nation have become increasingly crowded and violent in the last twenty years (Parent et al. 1994). Living in such stressful and crowded conditions encourages inmates to develop various coping techniques. While many of the techniques are extremely adaptive for prison life, some have a harmful impact on an inmate's relationship with his children. The first technique is called "hard timing."

Hard timing, according to the in-depth interview respondents, happens when inmates feel so overwhelmed by life in the institution that they cut off all ties to the outside world. They do this simply because it is too difficult for them to deal with problems inside and outside of the institution simultaneously. To illustrate the phenomenon of hard timing, I include two lengthy but illustrative quotes from the in-depth interviews. In response to a question asking what advice he would give to a father being sentenced to a few years in the CYA, Charles began to talk about the immense stress inmates feel:

> Some people get in there and it will be like a lot of problems from the outside coming in. They're constantly telling you about this problem, and mom's telling you about this problem, and then you got people you associate with, and you're having problems with another group or something. So you got all these problems coming at you at one time, you get so stressed out. So the first thing you do is you block your stress out

from the outside. . . . You try to concentrate on your living. It's just like survival skills, you know. If you're in the forest with a bear, the bear's attacking you but . . . you're trying to get back to Sacramento because somebody's in the hospital, you've got to deal with the bear first. So that's why people get caught up and cut off all the outside, and then they just call it "hard time." They just forget everything. They don't work on any mail, no phone calls. They're just hard timing.

Tyrell, a father of a two-year-old daughter, was incarcerated for over two years. He talked about hard time:

It be stuff like . . . they got family members dying and they not with their kids and their families, and then the holidays come and they're away, and they get stressed up, and you got so much on your mind to where you got to deal with all that stuff that's going on the outside and at the same time you have to deal with these 110, 120 people with different attitudes that's around you and then you have to deal with staff . . . and it's just like it's too much. To be honest, it's really too much.

Hard timing, as the young men describe it, is a reaction of stress to the prison environment. It also stems from men's guilt about their inability to support their families on the outside. Because most inmates are from the lowest economic classes, their families face the many hardships associated with poverty. In the parenting classes, I listened while the young men talked with each other about problems their families were facing. These stories frequently involved calamities such as being evicted from their homes, losing welfare benefits, and being victims of drive-by shootings. Not only do problems such as these continue while a young man is incarcerated; they sometimes increase in his absence. Incarcerated men hear about these problems and often feel guilty and powerless. As a result, some simply decide that it is easier not to know about the problems at all.

The structure of the prison encourages the hard-timing response because it provides few opportunities for inmates to help or support their families during times of crisis. I was told by staff that in the 1970s and 1980s there was much more flexibility in the rules applied to inmates whose families were undergoing difficult times. For example, inmates were sometimes allowed to attend funerals, albeit in handcuffs and accompanied by prison staff. Today, rules strictly forbid inmates to attend funerals or other important family events. The official rules also do not permit inmates extra telephone time or visiting hours at times of family crisis. Tony talked about his anguish when his great-grandmother died:

> At Preston, I was in the special program. . . . They wouldn't allow any spouses to come in. They would just allow family. Immediate family. There was one time my great-grandmother passed away and my sisters came to see me. My son's mother came with them, to give me support, and they wouldn't let them in. Them not letting them in on top of them taking the long trip from Sacramento to Ione was just hard for me to handle. I broke down for a couple of days.

When crises such as these do occur, the only way inmates can get special privileges is to appeal to the staff for compassion. A few young men, for example, told me that a staff member had let them make extra telephone calls at times of crisis. I also witnessed an exception being made for a young man at an institution I was visiting. His girlfriend had suffered a miscarriage and, although he was not supposed to see visitors other than his parents, the staff allowed him to spend a half hour with her. Because such exceptions are not built into the rules, however, they become a way for the staff to reward compliant young men.

Young inmates' guilt and powerlessness about their families often causes them to rely on hard timing as a coping strategy. Men who resort to hard timing cut off contact with their children as well as with the rest of their family. This causes them to miss out on key moments in their children's lives and may harm any bond they might have had. In addition, it is likely that hard timing causes resentment among family members which may hinder men's successful reintegration into family life.

Flashing: Teaching Inmates How to Control Behavior

If hard timing is a response to the highly stressful prison environment, "flashing" is a response to its punitive nature. In prison, rule infractions are dealt with swiftly and often harshly. The punishments employed are frequently arbitrary and have little relationship to the infraction committed. In a lawsuit filed against the juvenile justice system in Arizona, for example, the plaintiffs contended that punishments at the facilities were excessively harsh and were often inflicted as the result of "petty" infractions. Such punishments included leg shackles, handcuffs, and solitary confinement (Bortner and Williams 1997). Severe punishments, combined with the generally punitive nature of the institution, can have implications for young men as fathers.

The relationship between prison staff and inmates provides a potent model to undermine or enhance the parent/child relationship. The inmates, like children, have every aspect of their lives controlled. They are told when to sleep, eat, and watch television. The staff, who must maintain order and discipline, become the parents who "know best." The young men are exposed to a model of control maintained through fear and monitoring. As a result, the prison is, in effect, teaching men to use punishment as a way to manage their children. What follows is a quote from my parenting class field notes. That day, the discussion was about how prison shaped the men's behavior in their families once they were released. John is the instructor, and Carlos and Michael are two of the parolees in the class.

> Carlos says that guys learn to "flash" when they are upset about something with someone in their family. I ask what that means, and Carlos says that it is when they lose their tempers. Carlos says he learned this response in the institution. Michael is laughing and asks if they remember how the staff in the institution just used to flash. Carlos again says that you learn this in the institution—like somebody disrespects you and you just flash. Then your old lady does something and you flash. John wants to know what sets this off. Carlos says it might be because guys are sometimes jealous—like you'll be driving down the road and your old lady will be looking out the window and you look over and she is looking at some guy and you just blow up.

Flashing is one of the responses learned in punitive environments where people act out of frustration and a desire for retribution. It should, of course, be noted that even before coming to prison, many of the young men had violent tempers and many punished their children unduly. Some of them ended up in prison because of these problems. The important point, however, is that the punitive prison environment reinforces these traits. In the prison, there is no alternate model to that of rage, punishment, and hierarchy.

The California Youth Authority began providing parenting classes because they were concerned about parolees' tendency to flash and to punish their children harshly. They chose a curriculum that has as one of its major themes the ineffectiveness of punishment as a way to change behavior. In the words of the class text, "Consequences should enhance character and increase your child's options. Punishment erodes self-esteem and limits your child's character" (International Network for Children and Families 1994, 4–8). While the attempts of the CYA to teach about the dangers of punishment are admirable, they work against years of conditioning in an environment that uses punishment as its central tool for behavioral change.

Everybody's a Pimp:
Misogyny and the Gendered Nature of the Prison

One of the most obvious and least discussed characteristics of the prison system is that it generally adheres to a policy of segregation by sex. At the CYA, over 90 percent of inmates are male and, with one exception, all of the facilities are single gender. The gendered nature of the prison has profound implications for the male inmates' desire and opportunity to display their masculinity. Understanding prison masculinity is important because of its potential to affect inmates' relationships with their children and with their children's mothers.

In his work on masculinities, Robert Connell (1995) argues that it is not possible to identify a singular form of masculinity; the characteristics that define "masculinity" vary widely across time periods, cultures, and even from individual to individual. It is possible, however, to identify one model of masculinity that is held up as the cultural ideal at a given historical moment. Connell calls this ideal "hegemonic masculinity." Drawing on both Connell (1990, 1992) and Segal (1990), Messerschmidt (1993) suggests that hegemonic masculinity in the modern-day United States is defined "through work in the paid labor market, the subordination of women, heterosexism, and the driven and uncontrollable sexuality of men. . . . [It] emphasizes practices toward authority, control, competitive individualism independence, aggressiveness, and the capacity for violence" (82). Inherent in this definition is the idea that masculinity stands in opposition to both femininity and homosexuality—behaviors deemed appropriate for women and homosexuals serve as negative models for men (Connell 1995). Prison is a key location for the expression and reproduction of hegemonic masculinity because it is sex segregated and hierarchical (Sabo, Kupers, and London 2001).

When men enter prison, they bring the ideals of hegemonic masculinity with them, and they find themselves in an environment where the successful display of this masculinity is necessary for their survival. Prisons are extremely violent places—guards rule by the threat of violence, and violent acts between inmates are common. In a one-month period in 1991, for example, over 3 percent of all inmates in our nation's juvenile facilities were harmed by other inmates, and over 1.7 percent of staff were injured (Parent et al. 1994). To avoid victimization, inmates must quickly and continuously display "masculine" traits of toughness and violence; it is crucial that inmates do not appear feminine or homosexual in any way. Unfortunately, the structure of the prison leaves men few options besides violence for affirming their masculinity. They are not able to earn money, have a career, or have sex with women. As Newton (1994) comments, "The prisoner's masculinity is in fact besieged from every side: through loss of autonomy and independence, enforced submission to authority, lack of access to material goods, all of which are central to his status as a 'man'" (197).

In the face of an assault on their masculinity, prisoners rely on violence as a way to convince other inmates that they are appropriately masculine. Another method inmates employ is to speak in what is considered an appropriately masculine fashion. In prison, there are many opportunities for conversation; in fact, inmates have little else to do. As a result, talk becomes a central way to demonstrate masculinity—both talk about past sexual liaisons and negative comments about women. Of course, prisoners are not the only young men to use talk to assert their masculinity. Research with all-male adolescent groups outside prison demonstrates that misogynistic talk is common. For example, in Gary Allen Fine's study of Little League baseball (1987), he demonstrates that when pre-adolescent males spend time together they engage in talk that is "consistent with male domination and female submission" (110). Elijah Anderson (1990) documents how the denigration of women serves to unite groups of adolescent males. He shows that young men use tales of their sexual exploits with women as a way to elevate their status within the group. Wilson (1996, 99), in his work on the inner city, comments, "Males especially feel peer pressure to be sexually active. They said that the members of their peer networks brag about their sexual encounters and that they feel obligated to reveal their own sexual exploits." Wilson, Anderson, and Fine's work helps to confirm that prisoners are not unusual in their use of talk to assert masculinity. What makes prison talk different is the importance placed on it in the absence of other opportunities to express masculinity.

The paroled fathers spoke at length about how life in the institution enhanced misogynistic talk. For example, Charles said that at his prison:

> There's bad talk about women. Everybody in jail considers themselves; they think they're pimps; everybody got this many females; this is how they do it. People say, "Oh man, my girl, she crashed my car. I'm going to get somebody to beat her up. I'm going to do this to her and that to her." She'll say it's an accident, and you know it's an accident, but you know if you say that, somebody's going to outburst that they'd beat her.

Tony confirmed that the talk about women in the institution is highly negative.

> When a bunch of guys who really have nothing to do sit around, I don't know how it goes for females because I'm a guy, sometimes we have good conversations, but then most again we have conversations about

the worst ones. We hardly ever talk about the good ones because it makes you seem like you're not the stud, you're not the big time playboy that you want the appearance, you know what I'm saying. Just let the people in here that are married, they're happily married. But then there's others, you know, one of the playboys, and they had a reputation to mess with the most females, so most of the talk is negative. That's what most of the talk is.

Marco had a somewhat more balanced view. He felt that, while there was negative talk about women, not everyone participated in it:

> From different guys you hear different things. It matters what kind of guy it is, what kind of person he is, if he has respect for his girlfriends, or whatever, and he has respect for his mom and everything. You don't talk bad about women or girls, but some guys do. Whores, sluts, you know, I did this to 'em, I did that, whoop-de-whoop. Just telling stories. Make yourself look good or something, you know.

The talk that goes on in the institution is not significantly different from the talk among young males on the streets. What is different is the intensity of the talk and the fact that inmates have little contact with women (other than prison staff) who might have a counterbalancing influence.

The Summer Shake:
Fostering a Climate of Distrust of Women

Misogyny in the institution is not simply a result of men's need to assert their masculinity in an all-male environment. It also stems from threats to their masculinity coming into the institution from outside. Imprisonment fundamentally changes the power balance between men and their wives or girlfriends, and this is deeply upsetting to the men. In the outside world, men are fairly independent of women, and they pride themselves on being able to come and go as they please (Anderson 1990). They are able to monitor the behavior of their girlfriends and make sure that they are being faithful and are acting in what they consider to be an appropriate manner. The institution turns this power relationship upside down. Men suddenly become completely dependent on their wives or girlfriends. Women choose when and if they visit, and they have the power to withhold money, packages, and access to children. At the same time, the men are no longer in a position to monitor or control the women's behavior.

Inmates' inability to control their wives' and girlfriends' behavior causes them stress as they constantly worry that their girlfriends are seeing other men. These concerns are fueled by rumors they hear through the mail and during visiting hours. Friends and siblings gossip about their girlfriends' behavior. One young man told me that this happened frequently when he was in the institution. He said, "You might get a letter from your brother or your family member or friend or something, telling you they seen her do something here and there, and that they seen her with this different person or whatever. And it's like, you know, it's true." Another young man told me that he broke up with his girlfriend because he could not stand hearing rumors about her behavior:

> Me and my baby's mother had a problem 'cause I was locked up. She went out and did a couple of things and got me upset. So it's like I don't want a girlfriend which is doing this. So I had to let her go and tell her, "I can't be with you." When I'm with her, and I hear—like I'm locked up and I hear from my homeboys when I write them and they write me and tell me that my lady is kicking back with some homegirls, getting drunk or something, and I can't have that, so I let her go. So I tell my mom not to bring her, and she says she don't want to come, too.

Fueling the distrust of women caused by gossip from the outside, many stories of girlfriends' infidelity circulate within the institution. While some of these stories are certainly untrue, it is absolutely the case that large numbers of women actually do choose to terminate relationships with incarcerated men. The survey and in-depth respondents told me that many of their girlfriends tried to wait for them to be released from prison but eventually began to date other men. John told me about his breakup with his girlfriend:

> She had me fooled 'cause she had me thinking that she was going to be by my side the whole time and I was believing her and then I start noticing that—I mean, you could just tell that things had just changed. In the beginning with me it was a lot of letters—a real lot of communication—phone calls and everything. And then it started playing out real slow. It was playing out slowly but surely, and then at one point she wrote me a letter and said that she couldn't handle it because I had too much time and that she think that we should just break up right now and be friends.

The scenario John describes was so common that the young men in the institution called it "the summer shake." Tyrell told me what this meant:

> Like in the summertime, you know, all the girls get dressed up and go out and have fun. It's cool out. You know, it's summertime and they shake their boyfriends off. The summer shake. . . . We all used to make fun of each other. Like somebody's girlfriend stop writing them or whatever, and we'd say, "Ah, she gave you the summer shake!"

The large number of breakups in the already negatively charged prison environment further reinforces a deep distrust and anger toward women. Vance, a twenty-year-old white father of two children, whose relationship with the mother of his first child ended while he was incarcerated, told me what he learned in prison:

Just that all women are not any good and if you have a girlfriend out there, you know she's cheating on you, no matter what you think or what she tells you. She is, no matter what. We get that a lot. That they're all the same. You know, a lot of people—if you tell them you had a wife out there and you know she's faithful—they would laugh at you and diss you for believing that.

Men who hear the pervasive stories about women's infidelity sometimes choose to terminate their relationships with wives or girlfriends as a preemptive strike. Jeremy told me that he broke up with his child's mother when he learned he would be going to prison. He said:

When I go to jail, I don't have no girlfriend, okay. The girl's going to do what she's going to do. . . . I don't know what she's doing. So instead of me saying I've got a girlfriend, she's being good to me, and turn around and find out she cheated on me, just stress my mind out. So she's just my friend.

Jose, a twenty-three-year-old Latino father of a seven-year-old, talked about how he felt about his girlfriend the last time he was in prison:

All women tend to say, yeah, I'll be with you, be there for you, and they can't go through with it. Too much time goes by. They wanna have fun. They're young. They wanna go do things. They meet somebody they like. They leave. Like me, she left me like three weeks later. I was only gone for three weeks. Then she left me for some other guy she met at the movies. But that doesn't bother me, 'cause I can accept that, you know what I mean? That's reality. I knew for a fact that she was going to leave. Whatever she said in her letters didn't mean nothing.

The message that is constantly reinforced by the young men in the prison environment is that women are not to be trusted. One in-depth interview respondent revealed this attitude when I asked him what advice he would give to someone who was being sentenced to a few years in the CYA. He said, "Don't trust the baby's mom."

Mitigating Factors

For the most part, the prison environment and rule structure encourage young men to withdraw from their children and from their children's mothers. There are, however, countervailing tendencies in the institutional culture. Four factors that help men to be more responsible fathers are group support for active fatherhood, time to think, parenting classes, and educational programs.

Group Support for Active Fatherhood

In Goffman's work on institutional life (1961), he discusses the possibility of solidarity and support among the inmates of a total institution. He finds that friendships are possible but are usually limited by the institutional structure and by the staff's fears that friendships might be the basis for disruptive activities. Some of the research done since Goffman has provided support for this conclusion. For example, in a study of inmates in a federal narcotics hospital, Tittle (1972) found that there was little social organization. Bartollas, Miller, and Dinitz's work with juvenile inmates (1976) suggested that, while there was a clear social structure in the prison, it did not resemble social solidarity. Instead, it was a network of roles that served to exploit the weakest in the prison for the benefit of the few at the top of the power structure. Toch's study of a maximum security prison (1992) found that prisoners generally see other prisoners as "superficial" and "unhelpful" (79).

Research suggests that there are a number of reasons few friendships develop in prison. First, prisoners fear being labeled homosexual if they grow too close to another man. Sabo, Kupers, and London (2001) comment:

> Homophobia is a major obstacle to deep male/male friendship and to men's wholehearted participation in emotionally profound heterosexual intimacies. The guiding principle outside prison is "Don't do anything that might lead other guys to think you might be gay." So men do not hug or express much affection toward each other, except in those rare instances where such displays are condoned—for instance, a slap on the buttocks of a running back who just scored a touchdown. Men entering prison merely intensify their awareness about such principles. The new prisoner, if he is to survive, has to become especially vigilant, because the punishments for violating the code are much more drastic on the inside than on the outside. (10)

Along with fears about being labeled homosexual, prisoners also resist forming friendships because it can be dangerous. Derrick Corley, a writer and prisoner, comments, "Prisoners feel that it is better to keep one another at arm's length, not to get too close, for to get close opens up the possibility that somebody might be in a position to cause them harm" (2001, 106).

While inmate solidarity may be rare and difficult to maintain, there is some evidence that it does occur under certain circumstances. In a widely cited study of a prison in Illinois, Sykes (1958) found that considerable solidarity develops between inmates as a response to the deprivations imposed by prison structure. This social structure serves to allocate goods, disseminate information, and provide personal identity in the form of "argot roles" (unique roles corresponding to the social system within the prison). Corley (2001) argues that inmate friendships can occur either to provide protection or to pool scarce resources.

My discussions with the paroled fathers suggest that inmate solidarity can also be an important source of support. Fathers sometimes form a support system in the prison and encourage each other to be active participants in their children's lives. There are clearly exceptions to this rule; not all of the fathers are involved with their children nor do all of them support other fathers. For the most part, however, the in-depth interview respondents told me they felt free to talk about their children with other inmates and even to discuss problems they were having. Alberto said:

> Yeah, I always talk about my son, about how many months he is, about how long his hair is, how he still knows who I am and remembers me— and he knows I'm his father. Like, I kind of brag a little. He's my own little me. He's my son.

When asked if he talked with other men in the institution about his daughter, Charles responded:

> Always. . . . When you get a picture, everybody rushes to show each other a picture. They're always saying, "She's got your nose, she's got your eyes," just talking about it like that. And we'd be talking about what they're doing, talking about them to different parties and stuff.

Many of the fathers in the in-depth interviews told me that other inmates had encouraged them to be actively involved with their children. Vance commented:

> You see a lot of, like, if someone has two or three kids out there, and a lot of their friends or stuff in there will tell 'em, you should go out and be with your kids, you need to be there for them instead of being in here. It's rare you'd hear someone say something negative about someone else's kids or anything. Mostly people they know, kind of like everybody'll preach to everybody else. They need to know they don't do it themselves, so they tell everybody else what they should be doing, [that] they should be out there doing the right things for their family. Overall,

it's pretty good. The people know a lot of fathers, they get pictures of their kids once a month or twice a month, they always want to see 'em.

The support for being a father stands in startling contrast to the lack of support for maintaining relationships with women. Unfortunately, the two are intimately connected. Men who destroy their relationships with the mothers of their children are unlikely to see their children. We see this tension in comments made by Ray in response to my question about whether he spoke with other inmates about his son:

> The couple of guys that had kids could understand me, but the ones that didn't [would say], "Man, your baby's mother's gonna keep you broke and keep you with problems, always wanting you to baby-sit." They didn't understand. They were just all negative. She's going to take you to court and get you for all this money. At this time, money was everything to me.

Ray told me that he wanted to be involved with his son but that he grew increasingly distrustful of the child's mother. This obviously strained their relationship and made her less willing to bring the child to the prison. In the survey, I asked respondents about the factors influencing how often they saw their children in prison. The number one response was how well they were getting along with the mother of their child. A support system for fathers is of little use without an accompanying system of support for maintaining good relations with the mothers of their children.

Time to Think

While young men are provided some activities in prison, they also have a great deal of empty time. Much of this time is used imagining how their lives will be when they are released. They make plans and think about changes they want to make in their lives. The literature on adult prisoners suggests that this building of expectations is not unique to the juvenile population (McDermott and King 1992). Many of the fathers told me that their prison daydreams frequently revolved around their relationships with their children. They described how, when they were incarcerated, they anticipated being very involved and spending a lot of time developing a close relationship with their children. Marco described his image as follows:

> You picture it in your mind as good, great, you know. When you get out, man, you're going to love her, love them, do this with her and do that. Doing—you're always telling yourself, do things my parents never did with me, and give her everything she wants, just be so good to my daughter. And love her, tuck her in, read to her. So you picture it in your mind, and you imagine it in your mind to be great, to be wonderful.

Alberto, who was back in prison when he spoke with me, also talked about the high expectations he has for his future relationship with his son. He said:

> I think about it and picture it every day. You know, soon as I get out, I'll see my son and I'll just be able to be at home with him, you know, watch him run around, watch him get into trouble. . . . Just watch him grow up. Just be there for him.

In the next chapter I discuss what happens when the men's expectations meet the reality of the outside world. For the moment, it is simply important to understand that prison provides inmates with a period of time away from regular daily life. Many of the men use it as an opportunity to fantasize about how they would like to improve their relationships with their children.

Parenting Classes

The "Young Men as Fathers" Parenting Program was begun in 1993 as a pilot program at four CYA institutions, two in Northern California and two in Southern California. In 1995, Governor Pete Wilson became interested in the program and directed that it be extended to all CYA institutions and camps. The goal of the institutional parenting program is to promote active fatherhood by teaching young men parenting skills. Another goal is to decrease violence against children and to encourage young men to spend more time with their children.

Young men do not volunteer to take the institutional parenting classes; they are ordered to take them by a caseworker at the reception center, by the Parole Board, or by an intake worker at the institution. Fathers are given first priority for these classes, and young men who are father figures, or who are considered to be at "high risk" for fatherhood, are given second priority. About three-quarters of the young men in the survey sample were required to take one or more parenting classes at the institution. Most of the young men who did not take an institutional class either served time at an institution where the classes were not currently being offered or they were not yet fathers.

I asked the survey respondents to rate how helpful the classes were to them on a scale of 0 to 5, with 0 being "not at all helpful" and 5 being "extremely helpful." Over 45 percent of the sample reported that they found the class to be a 5. The average response was a 3.63. Only 11 percent of the men who took a parenting class rated it a 0. Perhaps the most compelling evidence for the positive effect of the classes comes from the comments made by many of the in-depth interview respondents. I did not ask them specifically about the classes, but frequently the young men brought up the topic themselves. Tony told me about how the parenting class he had taken in the institution helped him:

It helped me understand more what I was supposed to do. Because before I went to YA, I was just "I'm okay, I can get me some money, I can give her some money and buy clothes, and make sure she always got money," and that's all it took. You know . . . before I went to CYA, I didn't know nothing about the baby shaking syndrome or whatever. And I used to . . . like a little rough horseplay. I figure he was laughing; there wasn't nothing wrong with it. After going through that class, that's how a lot of babies are injured. Also, I know a lot of people who, before I went to YA, I used to do it, too, give babies alcohol to put them to sleep, and blowing marijuana smoke in their face, and I thought it was cool. I thought it was funny until I realized what could actually happen to the baby. Their system isn't as advanced as ours, you know. A little alcohol can kill a baby. I realize a lot about child safety. Being there for the child is more important than giving them money.

The in-depth interviews, as well as my observations in parole parenting classes, suggest that young men benefit from these classes because they are forced to think about fatherhood and to learn some alternatives to their old behavior patterns with their children. One of the most important messages given in parenting classes is that simply "being there" for children is key to their development. I include an extended quote from the evaluation report of the parole parenting classes:

In the interviews we asked the parolees what they learned from the class. Responses were varied, but three main themes emerge. The first is that the parolees learned the importance of spending time with their children. A number of students said that they never before thought about how important it is to spend time with their children. One student said, "[I learned] how to spend more time with my kids, you know. . . . That I need to spend a lot of time with my kids if you want them to be all right. If you want them to be good kids when they grow up, you have to spend time with them." Another student told the interviewer, "When the teacher told us to go spend time with our kids, I played Chicken Limbo with them. We played that for two hours. I had patience with them." The interviewer then asked him if it had been hard. He responded, "No, it was fun. It made me feel good. The kids were happy. It was better than watching TV." (Cohen et al. 1997)

Prison parenting classes provide important skills and thinking time for inmate fathers. Also, they support fathers for being involved with their kids.

Prison Educational Programs

All CYA institutions provide educational programs, and any inmate who has not completed high school is required to attend. The quality of the programs varies widely across the system, but most institutions provide at least minimal support to men trying to get a high school diploma or GED. In many institutions, men of all different levels are grouped together with one teacher, supplies are scarce, and books are often outdated. Understanding the effect of prison on a father's education is important because education is linked to later employment. As I discuss in the next chapter, employment improves a father's ability to provide financial support to his children.

Spending time in a CYA institution may affect a man's education in both positive and negative ways. For men who were regularly attending school prior to their incarceration, the effect is usually negative. Removal from the traditional school system disrupts the flow of their education. At the same time, many of the men who enter the Youth Authority have already dropped out of school.

For some of these men, prison education programs can be an inspiration to recommit themselves to getting a degree.

It appears that how men react to prison education varies greatly by where they serve their time. In the opinion of the paroled fathers, the best school in the system is the Ventura Training School in Southern California. As its name implies, the Ventura School is a special institution designed to help inmates with their educational and career goals. Most of the men who attended it spoke highly of its programs. A number of them commented that the education they received there rekindled their desire to learn. I spoke with Doug, who served most of his sentence at Ventura, about his educational experiences in the CYA.

A.N.: Did you get education [while in prison]?

Doug: Yeah. I received a high school diploma. . . . Yeah, and three semesters of college . . . through a community college.

A.N.: Did you do that when you were in or out?

Doug: In Ventura School, you could take college courses through there. That institution that I went to was co-ed. The only institution in all seventeen YAs or whatever that's co-ed. And you have to score high, and you have to have, like, high scores to be, to go there. It's like college courses, college programs. That was a good institution. . . . The college professors go into the YA. Every day they have, like, a school in there and at night the college professors use those classrooms. . . . I used to go every night for three or four hours, sit there in a room.

A.N.: Were the classes good?

Doug: Yeah, some were. I took music appreciation. It was cool. I learned how to play the piano, learn my notes. I took Chicano studies. Air and refrigeration. I just jumped around to a bunch of stuff because I never thought I was even going to make it there. And then I got out and I went to the Bakersfield College.

I asked Tony, who also attended Ventura, if incarceration had helped him in any way. He commented:

> Actually it has. Before I got incarcerated, I'd given up on school. Since I've been incarcerated, I'm concentrating on my GED, and now I'm more focused on school, because it helped me realize what I was doing out there, and that don't help me either way. So I'm going to change if I'm going to stay out there.

Tony's comments indicate that a strong academic program in prison can motivate young men who might otherwise drop out. Unfortunately, it appears that the Ventura School is an anomaly in the CYA System. The paroled fathers told me that the educational programs at most of the other institutions did little to inspire them to stay in school. I asked Jeremy how incarceration had hurt him. He told me, "I would, I don't know, probably more with my schooling. It hurt because you go to school, but you do the same thing over and over again." In response to a question about how incarceration had helped him, Paul echoed Jeremy's thoughts about the quality of the education at the Youth Authority. "There ain't really like no school. The schools are like continuation schools on the streets. You don't do anything. You just go there, sit there. They say, oh yeah, you can graduate or something like that."

Because I did not ask the paroled fathers about their educational experiences prior to their incarceration, I cannot make definitive statements about the impact of prison on their schooling. My experiences with them, however, suggest that when strong educational programs are offered in prison, they have the potential to reengage men with the educational system. Simply put, prison can serve as a turning point for men in their educational careers. On the other hand, when educational programs are poor and disorganized, men who already have a tenuous relationship with education may cut their ties entirely.

As illustrated here, there are various ways in which the juvenile prison experience shapes inmates' relationships with their children. The impact of incarceration on these relationships, especially the negative impact, is not intentional. The prison environment is structured with little regard for inmates who are fathers. In the chapters that follow, I consider the question of what effect, if any, the prison experience has on a man's relationship with his children once he is released.

3

Coming Home

> Although some roles can be re-established by the inmate if and when he
> returns to the world, it is plain that other losses are irrevocable and may
> be painfully experienced as such. It may not be possible to make up, at a
> later phase of the life cycle, the time not now spent in educational or job
> advancement, in courting, or in rearing one's children. (Goffman 1961,
> 15)

Young men leave prison and return home to find that many things
have changed in their absence. Girlfriends have moved on, friends
have new lives, and jobs once held are no longer available. Fathers
face particular challenges as they try to integrate themselves into
their children's lives. Most come home from prison with high
expectations for their own behavior and that of their children. As
described, many have spent hours in prison fantasizing about the
relationship they will build with their children. They imagine activities they will engage in together and how their children will act.
Central to this vision is the idea that their children will respond to
them as "daddy." This means that the children will recognize them
as fathers and will treat them with respect.

The returning fathers have dreams for themselves as well. Most
told me that when they left prison they were committed to becom-

ing a "good father" to their children. So many men told me that they wanted to be good fathers, I finally began asking them what they meant. While the question seemed to confuse some of them, most answered with a list of responsibilities they believed a good father fulfills. Below are a sample of the men's responses:

A.N.: What does a good father do in your opinion?

Jose: Set a good example and provide. That's a good father.

A.N.: Provide what?

Jose: Provide everything. Whatever that child needs to grow, mentally and physically. That's what I mean by providing.

A.N.: What does a good father do, in your opinion?

Randy: Why, a lot. They kind of forget about themselves and their needs, and worry about their child's needs and wants. And just focus everything on their kid, basically, and the relationship as the parent.

A.N.: What does a good father do?

Tyrell: Just love and be there for a child. All you can do is just love. Love is more than anything. Love is being there. Take the time to listen to them. Talk to them, understand 'em. That's a good father.

These quotes show that parolees envision the "good father" as a person who provides guidance, love, and financial support to his children. Most newly released fathers hope to assume all of these responsibilities. In this chapter, I explore what happens to the young fathers when they arrive home and face reality.

Coming Home to Children

Many of the paroled fathers told me that they left prison with a detailed vision of how their children would act. As the young men quickly discovered, however, their expectations had little basis in reality. Most of them had spent little or no time with their children and, consequently, had only a limited ability to imagine what their children would be like. Over 40 percent of the men's children were born while the men were incarcerated. Upon their release, some of the men had never met their children, and the others had interacted with them only during visiting hours. As a result, few were capable of forming a realistic picture of their children. Fathers who spent time with their children before being arrested were able to develop somewhat more realistic expectations, but they too operated with limited knowledge. The children they remembered from the time before their incarceration changed during their absence and, by the time the men were released, had entered entirely new developmental stages.

Because of their high expectations, the paroled fathers told me that when they first arrived home they were excited to see their children, and they made an effort to spend time with them. The first surprise many encountered was that their children did not recognize them. Over 34 percent of the men who had spent time in prison since the birth of their child agreed with the statement "Being incarcerated made your child forget you." Such an experience was deeply upsetting for the fathers, especially when they had spent time in prison thinking about how much their children would love them.

> A.N.: How did incarceration change your relationship with your daughter?
>
> Miguel: She knows who I am, she knows I'm her father, but I see it in her sometimes. She . . . feels I'm kind of a stranger in a way. She has that look in her eyes like she's kind of confused whether she should come and hug me. She treats me like a stranger sometimes 'cause she doesn't really know. . . . That hurts me 'cause I look at her like I'm her dad, you know.
>
> A.N.: Tell me about the first time you saw her when you got out.
>
> Miguel: It was weird because when she'd see me in the institution she

knew who I was—she was kind of running and giving me a hug. But when I got out that day I remember exactly—she looked at me like just stunned, like what are you doing here?

Randy told me about the first time he saw his son after he was released from prison. He was disappointed to find that the child seemed confused by his homecoming:

> Randy: It was weird. He didn't know what to do. And I didn't really know what to do either 'cause he was so much bigger. It was weird.
>
> A.N.: Where were you?
>
> Randy: Where was I when I first saw him?
>
> A.N.: Yes.
>
> Randy: I was at my grandma's house. She had to go pick him up because his mom still had the restraining order on me. He didn't really know what to say or do.
>
> A.N.: So what did you do?
>
> Randy: Try to play with him and fix him some food, and try to be a father.

I asked John to tell me about the first time he saw his daughter after he was released from prison.

> Well, her and her mother came over and I, I really, that was my first child, so I didn't really know nothing about being no dad. I knew I wanted to learn so when she first came over, because of me not seeing her, I didn't really know what to say, or what to do. So all I could say is like, "Come here," but I didn't really know what to say to her. She didn't want to come because she didn't really know who I was. Then her mother sat next to me and just held her and I was just talking to her and I was just trying to play with her, but I didn't really know what to say because this was my first time ever seeing her. I didn't know what to say or do.

These descriptions of homecomings illustrate the disappointment and confusion the men experienced when they arrived home to find that their children's reactions did not meet their expectations. Further compounding the problem, they reported that their children sometimes acted fearful or refused to obey. Of the 125 men who had spent time in prison since the birth of their children, 27 (15 percent) said that incarceration had made their child afraid of them. I asked Robert, an eighteen-year-old, about his transition home to his son. He told me, "Well, he'll sit there for a minute, he'll give me a hug, and I'll try to talk to him the best I could. But then he'll start looking for his mom, start getting anxious, then start to run away and start crying or something." While some children are afraid, others simply refuse to do what their fathers say. I asked Marco how his three-year-old daughter reacted the first few weeks he was out.

> Oh man, she didn't know me. You know, it was like if I told her any-thing, she didn't know whether to listen to me or run away from me. She still knew who I was, so when I came, she greeted me, gave me a hug and a kiss, and whatever, but when it came to listening to me or, you know, if I told her something, she didn't know how to act either. And I didn't know how to act whether, by telling her no, or you know, I wasn't really in that position to tell her no, because she didn't really know me.

Like Marco, Doug told me about child discipline problems he encountered in the months after his release from prison. In response to a question about how his son acted, Doug said, "Him talking back to me. Me trying to discipline him. He doesn't listen. Just if I tell him something, he'll right away say no. I've never been there . . . so he's just not used to me telling him what to do. . . . If I tell him something he gets mad, runs to his mom and says daddy is being mean or whatever. But I was never—I was gone for . . . just two years."

One of the reasons young men come home to find their children confused and disobedient is that other people have come to fill the "father" role in their absence. Jose commented on how frequently this occurs.

> When a kid doesn't see their father, original or real father, they tend to latch on to whoever is next to them, you know what I mean? If her mom has a new boyfriend, that's "daddy." . . . I mean, I see it every day. When somebody gets locked up, what we call Sancho—you know, sidekick— that's the next dude in line—takes over and raises the kid with the kid calling him "dad."

Many of the paroled fathers told me stories of "Sanchos." Robert reported that while he was incarcerated, his brother became like a father to his child. "He called my brother "dad," "daddy," one time. And I was like, man—you know, 'cause he was there for him as much as possible or whatever." I asked him how he had felt when his child called his brother "daddy." "I was hurt bad, bad." Randy told me that, during his incarceration, his grandmother had taken over as the principal person in his child's life:

> It's kind of weird, but it's uncomfortable for me when my grandmother's around because I feel like my son forgets about me. Because he was so attached to her when I was gone. And she gave him more than 100 percent of her attention. It's like she just dropped everything and did nothing but play with him all day. Twenty-four hours a day, seven days a week, all she did was play.

Alberto, who was out of prison for only twenty-one days before being arrested again, said that his time at home with his son had been upsetting:

> I felt kind of messed up 'cause when I had got out, it's like my little brother, it's like he was going to my little brother a lot, too. I'd be carry-

ing him and he'd see my little brother and it's like . . . I felt like my little brother was a dad and I'm like, "I feel bad," you know. . . . My son probably think that he's his dad now.

From these quotes it is clear that paroled fathers, most of whom have built up high expectations for being a daddy, are deeply disappointed and jealous of the new father figures in their children's lives. The weight of these problems and tensions, combined with the disappointment of unfulfilled expectations, can lead men to withdraw from their children.

Coming Home to Themselves

Paroled fathers often face disappointment when they return home and find that their children's behavior fails to meet their expectations. In some cases, however, the men's inability to live up to their own expectations causes even more disappointment. The paroled fathers told me that one of their primary goals upon their release was to obtain employment and begin to support their children. The importance that the men placed on providing for their children is not unique to paroled fathers—researchers working in the more general population of fathers have found that men often see financial support as one of the key components of responsible fatherhood (Cazenave 1979; Roy 1999). Because of their desire to fulfill the "good provider" part of fatherhood, many of the paroled fathers told me that they began to look for a job soon after they were released.

Most of the paroled fathers' hopes for quickly finding employment faded as they encountered the realities of the job market. Due to low levels of education—only half had completed high school—the men were only qualified for entry-level and unskilled jobs. Unfortunately, these were exactly the same jobs that were most diffi-

cult to find in the late 1990s. William Wilson's study of employment in the inner city (1996) showed how decreasing numbers of
blue-collar jobs resulted in a very tight labor market for unskilled
jobs. In an intensive four-city survey of employers, Harry Holzer
(1996) also found that there are few jobs available for people without a college degree, particularly in the central cities. Those jobs
which are available pay little and often require skills that many
low-income applicants do not have.

Given these facts about the labor market, it is not surprising that
40 percent of the paroled fathers were unemployed at the time of
the survey. While it is likely that this high level of unemployment
was primarily a result of the large-scale economic forces identified
by Wilson and Holzer, it is also important to acknowledge that the
men's criminal histories probably played a role. A criminal record
is one extra obstacle preventing men from competing effectively
for the few available jobs. It is only logical that an employer choos-
ing between many equally qualified young people would prefer
those without criminal histories. Holzer's interviews (1996) with
employers verified this preference. Only 30-35 percent of the employers reported that they would consider hiring someone with a
criminal record. This compared with the 81-86 percent who would
consider hiring a welfare recipient and the 67-68 percent who
would hire someone who had been unemployed for a year.

Although they do need to answer truthfully if asked, paroled
men do not have a legal responsibility to volunteer information
about their parole status to potential employers. Some parolees,
however, find that they need to reveal that they have been to prison
in order to explain where they completed high school or why they
have no previous job experience. Sometimes a young man without
an employment record has no option but to list his parole agent as
a character reference. Other young men must tell potential employers that they have been to prison because of parole restrictions lim-

iting the hours they can work. Scott had a great deal of trouble finding a job. "When you write 'parole' (on the application), most people . . . won't even give you no time of day at all. I mean, most places I've been to won't even talk to me." I asked him if he had to tell potential employers that he was on parole. He responded, "You're supposed to if they ask you, but I've been leaving, like the place I just got hired on, I left it blank. I didn't write yes or no. I just left it blank. And they hired me."

Not all of the problems parolees have finding a job can be traced to employers' reluctance to hire men on parole. In truth, some of the young men harm their own chances of getting a job because they have tattoos or they dress in a way that implies they are gang members. Further, the personality changes that accompany incarceration (described in chapter 2) hurt some of the men's ability to find employment. Charles told me how his own negative and distrustful attitude was contributing to his inability to get a job.

> You know, you can't trust nobody [in the institution], so when you get out on the streets you have your guard up all the time, you know. Somebody could really be coming with a real proposal to you, a job opportunity or just anything, and you'll always have your doubts. Which is good, but you'll always have your doubts, and you might not be paying attention because you think they're trying to gang you or something. I just feel you're always on the defensive side, you know. You just feel like you lower yourself. You feel downgraded. When you get out, you fill out an application for a job, you've always got that doubt in the back of your head they ain't going to hire you. You know, stuff like that. It could lower your self-esteem with that label you got to hold over your head when you get out.

Men who appear to be in a gang, who have a bad attitude, or who dress poorly have difficulty finding employers willing to hire them. The fact remains, however, that many of the parolees do everything right and still fail to find work. I saw many cases of young men who were making every effort to find a job but were unable to obtain one. For example, I attended parenting classes with a young man who had been out on parole for a number of months and was actively seeking work. He spoke well, attended parenting classes faithfully, and dressed neatly. What follows is an excerpt from my field notes. Carl is the parolee attending the class, and John is the teacher.

> Before class started, the teacher was mostly talking to Carl (young man who lives with girlfriend's child). He is trying to get a job—any kind of job seemingly—but is not having any luck at all. John started lecturing about the proper way to dress, but Carl said that he had been dressing up—with "dress shoes"—and that he had even gotten a haircut, which he had not wanted to do, that cost him $10. He thinks that it is his parole record that is precluding him from getting a job. He applied to Vons and a number of other places. John argued that it was a tight job market in the city. Carl mentioned that he had robbery on his record and they wouldn't let him work the cash register.

My experiences in the parenting classes suggest that Carl's situation is not unusual; there were frequent discussions of men's difficulties finding employment. In one class, the teacher asked the parolees to report on their employment prospects each week. Week after week, the men reported that they had found nothing. Many seemed to be holding out hope for summer "youth corps" jobs, but it was never entirely clear where or when these jobs would be available.

While unemployment was a serious problem for many of the paroled fathers, the majority did find work eventually. These jobs were located almost exclusively in the low-wage sector, with the most common jobs being fast-food worker, auto detailer, and landscaper. The median hourly wage was $6.17. Over 35 percent of the employed men in the survey held part-time positions, although virtually all said that they would like full-time work. Most of the men moved frequently between jobs, with periods of unemployment. On average, the employed men in the survey had been at their current jobs for fifteen weeks, and those who were unemployed reported that their most recent job lasted an average of twelve weeks. These low-paying and unstable jobs meant that the men had only a limited ability to contribute money toward the support of their children. Their employment, however, did allow them to contribute more than their unemployed counterparts. The employed men reported that they gave an average of $50 a month more than the amount reported by unemployed fathers. Employed men were also more likely to provide consistent support to their children: 79 percent of the employed men and 59 percent of the unemployed said they provided monetary support "regularly" as opposed to "just sometimes." Not surprisingly, the employed men also reported that in the month preceding the survey, they provided food, diapers, and clothing twice as often as did the unemployed men.

While employment made monetary support possible, it also sometimes had the ironic effect of decreasing the paroled fathers' ability to fulfill the other aspects of the "good father" role. Specifically, some of the working fathers had schedules that made it difficult for them to see their children. Over half of the employed men in the survey told me that they worked irregular schedules—often rotating between shifts. This type of variation in work hours made it hard to establish a regular schedule for seeing children. Related to this, some of the working men had complex lives, juggling multiple jobs, school, and obligations to the parole office. As part of the survey, I asked the nonresident fathers about the effect of their work, school, and parole commitments on the amount of time they spend with their children. About 45 percent reported that there was a conflict that sometimes caused them to reduce the time they spend with their child. This was particularly true for the 20 percent of the fathers who combined one or more jobs with being a student. One of the in-depth interview respondents, Tony, fell into this category. I asked him to tell me about how having a child had changed his life.

> It's kind of hard for me to answer that question 'cause I was so young when he was born. Before he was born, my life was go to school, come home, do homework, go to school, come home, do homework. And then he's born, and then I got a whole different life. I got to take care of my kid twenty-four hours a day, seven days a week, go to school, come home, do homework, clean the house, cook dinner, cook food, you know, all kinds of stuff. So I don't know. It's real hard.

Eventually Tony could no longer handle the strain of school, work, and childcare, and he decided to drop out of school. Other men in similar situations found that it was easier to postpone or cancel their time with their children than it was to change their work or school schedule. When the choice was between losing a job and missing a visit with a child, the job often had to take first priority.

Paroled fathers are not much different from fathers without criminal histories. Most share the same hopes for being close to their children, and they accept popular norms dictating the role of the "good father." In accepting these norms and hopes, however, paroled fathers often set themselves up for failure. High levels of unemployment, unstable and low-level jobs, and limited education ensure that most will never be able to attain enough financial stability to fulfill the "good father" duty of providing regular support to their children. At the same time, those who do find work may not have enough time to give the love and guidance that the role also entails.

"The Most Important Thing":
Continuing Good Intentions for Involvement

Given the difficulty newly released men face in reestablishing relationships with their children, one might expect them to lower their desire for involvement. I did not find this to be true, however. In my interactions with the paroled fathers, I found that even those who had been out of prison for several years spoke enthusiastically about their desire to be actively involved with their children. Almost uniformly, they told me that they wanted to support their children and maintain a relationship with them. As part of the in-depth interviews, I asked the respondents to think about all the things that were important to them and to rate the relative importance of their relationship with their child. Almost every father said that his child was "the most important thing" in his life or that the child was "extremely important." I asked Doug to talk about the importance of his relationship with his son.

> Doug: So important that I won't ever make those stupid mistakes again. I won't. I won't jeopardize it. I won't do it again. I'm just too mature now. My kids mean, especially Doug Jr., he means more to me than anything. I won't go out and steal no more. I won't go out and do stuff like that 'cause I know that if I get caught I'm going to go to jail. And I won't jeopardize that.
>
> A.N.: What do you want in your relationship with Doug Jr.?
>
> Doug: I want a good relationship. And I want him to be honest with me. And I want him to trust me. I want to be able to trust him. As he gets older, I just want to be there for him. I just want to show him that I'm his dad and that I'm responsible for him and that I can be there for him.

In response to the same question, Tony said, "I'm going to have years and years to teach him, you know, support him. My whole life, my focus is going to be on him and his siblings. My other children. That's the most important."

While most of the men, like Doug and Tony, talked about commitment to their children, it would be naïve to consider these remarks alone as accurately reflecting their feelings. It is likely that some of their enthusiasm about fatherhood was an effort to portray themselves in a positive light. More compelling evidence of men's interest in their children came from my observations in parenting classes. The young men in these classes had not volunteered to be there; they were forced to attend by their parole agents, and many of them were extremely resentful. It was fascinating, however, to watch how even the most reluctant would suddenly pay attention when something was being said that was relevant to their children. They were eager for an opportunity to talk about their children and to learn techniques helpful in handling the different stages of childhood. In one class session, for example, a young man seemed distracted and upset. Finally he raised his hand and told us that he was worried because his child often vomited after eating. We spent a good part of what turned out to be a highly participatory session discussing solutions for his problem. Incidents like this were more common in some classes than others, but were far from infrequent. It was clear that most of the men wanted to be involved with their own children and that they supported other fathers in their efforts.

The paroled fathers told me that their desire to be involved with their children was motivated by a number of factors, including love for their children and a belief that it was the right thing to do. Many remembered growing up without their own fathers. While half of the survey respondents reported that they had lived with their biological fathers for five years or more, only 30 percent lived with them for the duration of their youth (until they turned eighteen or, in the case of sixteen- and seventeen-year-old respondents, until the time of the survey). About 15 percent had never lived with their fathers. Many of the men whose fathers were absent during their childhood expressed anger and resentment toward the fathers for not being there while they were children. Robert's father was sent to prison for a number of years; once he was released, he rarely came to visit.

> He still didn't make any kind of contact, but he wouldn't try, wouldn't try to come visit us or call or nothing. And then even when we got older, he wouldn't even attempt. And that's what hurt, you know, hurt and made me angry.

Alberto expressed similar feelings about his father:

> I love him 'cause he's my father, but I hate him because he's never there for me. He just left me hanging. I was eleven years old when he left. He was always making me go to church and I was going with him to work to help him sell things, but he would never communicate or tell me to do the right thing. Sometimes he'd be like, "Don't get into trouble. Have a nice day," and that's it. 'Cause my dad, he was an alcoholic and a drug addict.

In the survey I asked all of the young men to rate the relationship they had with their father when they were growing up. They were instructed to use a scale from 0 to 5 in which 0 was "extremely poor relationship" and 5 was "extremely good relationship." One-third of the respondents rated their relationship a 0 and half ranked their relationship as a 2 or less. Only 18 percent rated the relationship as a 5.

The fact that many paroled fathers had weak or nonexistent relationships with their own fathers led them to create an idealized image of what a father should be. This ideal was based on their own fathers as negative role models. I asked Tony what he had learned from his father.

> Actually, my father, he tried to be there for me, but he just wasn't. He wanted to be, but he wasn't. He had a lot of problems with himself. You know, the thing he did teach me was not to let anything else interfere with your father/child relationship, because he had problems with women in his life, after him and my mother, the women in his life, they were more important than I was. So even if my son's mother and me never get back together, no one else in my life is going to be closer to me than my son is, as far as spousewise. They'll never be as close to me as my child.

Sam talked at some length about the importance of maintaining a relationship with his daughter.

> That's very important to me. That's like one of the most important things that I think about. Because like I said, I didn't have a father for me when I was younger, you know what I'm saying? And I still don't. And I don't want my daughter growing up without a father. . . . 'Cause then she'll feel neglected. She'll grow up with the same anger that I did.

During the years I spent working with the paroled fathers, it became apparent that most of the men, like Sam, had very good intentions for involvement with their children. These intentions were based on love for the children themselves and, for some, on resentment toward their own absent fathers. I turn now to the question of whether these good intentions actually translated into action.

Actual Involvement with Children

Measuring the extent of the paroled fathers' involvement with their children proved to be a greater challenge than I expected. Because there are so many ways that men can play a role in their children's lives, it is hard to define involvement broadly enough to capture its many aspects. At the same time, I needed to define it narrowly enough to make its measurement on a survey possible. In public discourse, we tend to measure the involvement of young fathers by one marker—the amount of child support they pay. The problem with this focus is that it blinds us to other ways in which men are involved with their children. Many fathers, for example, pay child support but do not do so through the formal child support system. Some also provide diapers, food, and clothing for their children. Some spend time with their children. Reducing father involvement to formal child support is misleading and underestimates the true levels of men's involvement with their children.

In the sections that follow, I divide father involvement into three categories: formal child support, informal/in-kind support, and visitation. For my discussion of the last two categories, I focus on the 70 percent of the paroled fathers who were not living with their children. I made this decision because living with a child is the most consistent and reliable predictor of all measures of involvement. In the survey, the resident fathers reported the highest levels of every kind of interaction with their children including playing with them, changing their diapers, and providing financial support. My focus on nonresident fathers is based on the fact that their involvement with children is much more varied and complex than that of the resident fathers.

Formal Child Support

In recent years, policymakers have begun to focus on increasing both the number of child support orders for children in single-parent homes and the number of fathers who comply with those orders. These efforts are in response to data suggesting that only 60 percent of households with absent fathers have a child support order (DiNitto 1995, 170). Because the establishment of child support orders for out-of-wedlock births involves two separate legal processes, it will likely be difficult to increase this figure.

Paternity establishment is a process through which out-of-wedlock fathers are formally recognized and gain some legally protected rights over their children. Child support cannot be collected from men unless paternity has been established. In recent years researchers have conducted some of the first studies to look at paternity establishment. The findings consistently show that paternity is established in only one-third of out-of-wedlock births. Studies also show that young, low-income men have little understanding of paternity law, and most do not consider legal paternity establishment a particularly important component of fatherhood (Sullivan 1993; Waller 1995; Wattenberg, Brewer, and Resnick 1991). Wattenberg (1993) identified a number of factors that increase the likelihood of a young man declaring paternity. These include education, employment, having had his father present during his own childhood, having a good relationship with the mother of his child, and having friends who encourage taking responsibility for the child.

In California, paternity is automatically assigned at the birth of a child to the mother's husband. In cases of out-of-wedlock births, it is established when a man signs a set of forms declaring that he is the father of the child. Contrary to popular belief, paternity is not established by simply putting a name on the birth certificate. When a man is served with paternity papers, he can voluntarily sign them or he can request a blood test to verify that he is the father. California has recently implemented a rule that requires any woman applying for Aid to Families with Dependent Children (AFDC) to identify her child's father. In theory, the Family Support Division, to whom this report is submitted, then locates the man, establishes paternity, and orders child support payments.

Young fathers on parole are frequently confused about what paternity establishment is and how it relates to their child support obligations. This makes it difficult to estimate the number of fathers with legally documented paternity status. One of the reasons for confusion is that much of the paroled fathers' knowledge seems to come from rumors they hear on the street. What follows is a fairly typical response to my inquiry about paternity establishment.

> A.N.: Did you sign any paternity papers?
> Tyrell: No.
> A.N.: How did you get out of that?
> Tyrell: I don't know. Things I buy for my daughter I keep all my receipts so in case they do try to come to me, like "you owe us money, you haven't been taking care of your daughter," I have all these receipts for all these things.
> A.N.: How did you know to do that? I never would have thought of that.
> Tyrell: Just listening to other people, my friends. The older ones, they like, "I had a baby by her, and a baby by her, then a baby by her, then John Phillips he hit me." So I started keeping receipts.
> A.N.: John Phillips?
> Tyrell: Yeah, that's the DA for child support.
> A.N.: Is that a person's name or an expression?
> Tyrell: That's his name. Everybody talks about John Phillips.

It is clear from this quote that Tyrell does not understand what I mean by paternity establishment; he confuses it with child support payment. While the two are obviously connected, they involve separate legal processes. This kind of confusion about paternity establishment is not unique to the paroled father population. Wattenberg (1993) also found that the young fathers in her study had an incomplete understanding of the process of declaring paternity.

Although self-report data on paternity establishment are somewhat unreliable, I did ask the survey respondents who had children out of wedlock if they had signed any papers, besides the birth certificate, saying that they were the father. About 40 percent told me that they were fairly certain they had done so. Given the age and education level of the paroled fathers, this figure is higher than might be expected. A combination of factors may help to explain this relatively high paternity-establishment rate among parolees. First, incarcerated men are easy to locate. About 23 percent of all those who signed papers were found by the Family Support Division when they were in correctional institutions. Second, it is likely that the new welfare-reporting law in California is contributing to an increase in the number of paternity establishments. The fact that over 14 percent of the young men who signed papers did so at the welfare office indicates that this may be the case.

I asked the survey respondents who had signed paternity forms whether they had done so voluntarily or been forced to do so by the district attorney or by a court. Only 10 percent told me that they were forced to sign the papers. It should be noted, however, that of the "voluntary" paternity establishments, most happened after a child's mother applied for welfare or requested a child support order. The fathers may not have fought the establishment of paternity, but they did not seek it out either. Seventeen men actively sought out the forms in order to get custody of their children.

Paternity establishment is important because it grants men legal rights over their children and it paves the way for the establishment of a child support order. Given the low rate of paternity establishment among parolees, it is not surprising that very few are legally obligated to pay child support. Only 19 percent of the survey respondents said that they had child support orders for their oldest child. These orders ranged from $25 a month to $640 a month, with an average award of $184 a month. Of course, the establishment of a child support order does not guarantee that the child will actually receive any funds. Estimates suggest that among men who are obligated to pay child support, under 30 percent pay the full amount ordered (DiNitto 1995, 170). This compliance is even lower for poorly educated, low-income, unemployed, and minority males (Committee on Ways and Means 1993; Danziger and Nichols-Casebolt 1990), but rates of compliance are particularly low for adolescent fathers of all races (Pirog-Good and Good 1995).

While we see low rates of compliance among paroled fathers, they are higher than the research just cited might lead us to expect. About 40 percent of the paroled fathers reported that they paid in full each month. Another 40 percent said that they did not pay any money at all. The rest either paid part of their payment each month or they paid some months and not others. The higher rates of child support payment, for parolees as compared with young fathers in the general population, is probably a function of their greater involvement with the state. Because they are on parole, state authorities know where the fathers are, and they are able to threaten the men with violating parole if they do not pay their child support.

In the survey, I asked men why they did not pay any or all of their child support. The most common answer was that they did not have enough money. A second, and related, reason was that they believed their payment was unjustifiably high. Randy told me that he had a minimum-wage job and was struggling to pay both his monthly support and a delinquent amount the county calculated he owed:

> When I was incarcerated I got served with child support papers. Now I'm paying $179.00 a month for one child. And almost $3,000.00 in back child support. . . . [The] back stuff they said I owe because, I don't even understand why they're saying I owe it, because when me and my son's mom were together and I was employed, I would send in my check stubs to the office and they would deduct a certain amount of money off

the check, depending on my income, and the case worker said that that was so in the future, they didn't charge me for back child support. Well, they're doing it anyway. So I guess I paid twice for it.

Randy is fairly representative of men who do not pay their full amount of child support. Over 36 percent told me that their non-compliance was, at least in part, because they believed they were being overcharged. Men who provide material goods for their children feel particularly resentful of high child support payments. Charles felt he took care of all of his daughter's material needs, but he was still required to make his child support payment. He told me how he felt about child support:

> When she was needing Pampers, I kept in the closet a stack with Pampers, baby wipes. . . . She was getting an allergic reaction to Similac, so I had to buy all milk. So I'm a provider for my daughter either way, whether I got to pay you guys [the Division of Family Support], I'm going to do for my daughter either way. But that's extra money I'm giving them for nothing, you know."

Anger about the amount of child support is only one of the reasons men fail to pay. Some refuse to pay because they know that their support payment is subtracted from the amount of the welfare check given to their child's mother. About 36 percent of non-compliers said that it seemed pointless to pay the money through the organized system if it would not increase the mother's total monthly income. Another reason men gave for not paying their child support was that they feared the child's mother had too much discretion over how the money was used; instead of spending it on the children, they felt she might spend it on herself. Hernaldo, a twenty-year-old Latino father of a five-year-old, was grudgingly paying his support but said: "Oh, yeah. If I was to give her the money and handle it like that, I feel that she wouldn't spend it on the kid. She would spend it on herself, you know. And so now, the stuff I'm paying back now, she's gonna get a check, but I feel that she don't—I don't know if she is or not going to buy stuff for the kids, you know. I will never know." This type of concern about how mothers spend money is far from universal among parolees, but it is also not unusual. About 13 percent of the noncompliers justified not paying child support because they do not trust the mothers to spend the money on the children.

As all of this evidence suggests, a good number of the paroled fathers harbor hostility toward the organized child support system. Many believe that men should support their children on their own, without the interference of the government. Exploring this topic, I asked all of the survey participants to respond to two attitudinal statements about child support: "I would be very angry if the mother of my child got a legal order saying that I had to pay child support," and "It should be the government's job to make sure that men support their children." Over half of the men agreed that they would be "very angry" if the mother got an order against them. About 60 percent disagreed, or strongly disagreed, with the statement that child support should be the government's responsibility. It is not surprising that this particular group of young men, who have a great deal of direct and negative experience with the legal system, would be opposed to government intervention in any area of their lives.

Research with young fathers in the general population suggests that resentment about the amount of child support payments is not confined to parolees (Furstenberg, Sherwood, and Sullivan 1992). Paroled men, however, do face unique circumstances that seem to make their resentment particularly acute. In California, fathers are not supposed to accrue child support payment obligations while they are incarcerated. Unfortunately, there is no communication between the California Youth Authority and the Division of Family Support, so there is no way for Family Support to know that the fathers are incarcerated unless the young men or their families inform them. The majority of the young men in the sample had low levels of education, and few had any previous positive experiences with the law. As a result, many of them did not know their legal rights, nor did they feel they had the power to protest their rapidly mounting bills. The young men who did try to confront the Division of Family Support did so with mixed results. Some told Family Support that they were incarcerated and received word back that their debts had been erased. Most, however, were not able to reduce their debt. Jeremy's situation was fairly representative:

> The first time I got served with 'em, I was in the county jail. And they called me out and they gave me some papers. They're like, "Here's some child support papers. You've been served," . . . and they're like, "Are you the parent?" and I'm like, "Yeah." . . . So I signed it off. And then I went to YA, and while I was there, they kept sending me bills for child support, $170 each month. And I would write to 'em and explain to 'em I'm incarcerated, I have no way to pay it, I'm not employed. They never responded. They just kept sending me more and more bills. Then I had my parole agent call, and he called and left a message for them to contact him, but they never did. . . . They just kept sending [the bills]. Right now it's like $6,500.

Out of the 188 young men in the survey who spent time in prison since the birth of their child, 35 (19 percent) had legal child support orders established before or during their incarceration. All were charged for the months they were incarcerated, but eleven took successful legal action to have their debt erased or reduced. Three men took unsuccessful legal action, and two cases were still pending at the time of the survey. The other nineteen men did not take any action to have their debts reduced, and most owed thousands of dollars for the time they spent in prison. When I spoke with them about their debts, many of the nineteen men reported that they felt angry and helpless to do anything to lower the amount they owed.

While debts that accrue during incarceration anger men and discourage their compliance with child support payments, time in prison can also help men establish a relationship with the child support system. Prisoners are easy to locate for the purpose of establishing orders, and they can receive help with the paperwork from YA staff. About a quarter of the survey respondents who had children reported that they received legal documents regarding those children while they were in prison. About 88 percent of these papers involved the establishment or adjustment of a child support order. Other men received documents involving child custody, termination of parental rights, welfare restitution, and paternity establishment. About 60 percent of the survey respondents who received papers reported that they had trouble understanding them. Paul told me that he had gotten papers in the mail several months previously. I asked him what the papers involved. He said: "I don't know. I received one set of papers. . . . So I read it, but I don't know what it meant. So, in truth, I can't read good. I can do math, but I can't read good. I don't really know what those papers mean. They are just giving me papers, and they think probably I'm like a lawyer. I don't know what all these codes mean."

When men are in prison and find that they cannot understand legal papers, they are often able to avail themselves of the help of the staff. Close to 50 percent of the respondents who received legal documents said that they sought out and received help from a CYA staff person. Only 20 percent said that there was no staff member available to help. Men who are out in the community when they receive their documents are less likely to have the resources or the knowledge required to find help.

Informal Child Support and Nonmonetary Support

While young paroled fathers have low rates of involvement with the legal child support system, most said that they provide money to their children informally. About 80 percent reported that they gave money to their children at least occasionally. The support, however, was not consistent; only 30 percent of those who gave money said that they did so on a regular schedule. Of those men who provided sporadic support, most said they gave money based on how much they had and on their child's needs in any given week or month. About 15 percent reported that they gave support based on how well they were getting along with the child's mother.

In addition to contributing money, the nonresident fathers reported that they provided material support. Most (65 percent) reported that they had given food, diapers, or clothes to their oldest child in the previous month. Of these young men, close to 50 percent estimated that they contributed these goods once or twice during the month; the rest said that they bought items for their child even more frequently.

Based on stereotypes, one might expect to find racial and ethnic differences in how much involvement young paroled fathers have with their children. These stereotypes portray black fathers as particularly irresponsible, impregnating multiple women and leaving them to fend for themselves. While this image suggests that black fathers would be less involved with their children than whites, the paroled fathers' reports point to the opposite reality: Black fathers report being much more involved in the lives of their children than do the white fathers. This difference is consistent across various types of involvement. In terms of in-kind support, the black men were more likely than whites to report that they had bought their child diapers, clothes, or food in the last month (74 percent of blacks and 36 percent of whites).[1] Latinos were also more likely than whites to report providing nonmonetary support. About 69 percent of the Latino survey respondents reported that they had bought their child diapers, clothing, or food in the previous month.

Visitation

Perhaps the most important indicator of a paroled father's involvement with his children is how often he sees them. Spending time with children is not dependent on having money, nor does it require involvement with the legal system. Because parolees generally have very little income and harbor deep fears about interacting with the legal system, visitation is one of the few ways they can be involved with their children. I asked all of the survey respondents who were not living with their children how often they saw them. More than 21 percent of the nonresident fathers reported that they saw their oldest child every day; 15 percent said that they had no direct contact. Another 49 percent said that they spent time with their children every week. There were, however, important racial/ethnic differences in how often the paroled fathers reported seeing their children. The black survey respondents, for example, reported that they saw their children more often than did their white counterparts. On a 6-point scale of father/child contact with 1 representing no contact and 6 representing daily contact, blacks scored an average of 4.28 points and whites 2.82 points. The finding that black nonresident fathers from my sample visit more often with their children than do whites is consistent with research conducted in the more general population of young fathers (Lerman 1993; Mott 1990; Sullivan 1993).

Turning to Latino fathers, we see that their reported level of involvement with their children is similar to that of the black fathers. The average Latino father/child contact score was 4.23 out of 6. This figures must be read with some caution, however, because father/child visitation is one of the areas where there is diversity among the Latino paroled fathers. Latinos with a foreign-born parent scored, on average, 4.54 on the contact scale (n=39) while those whose parents were native-born scored an average of 3.91 (n=41).[2] It would appear that nonresident fathers' contact with children decreases with each succeeding generation in the United States.

Exploring paroled fathers' patterns of visitation with their children is particularly interesting because parolees spend time with children under unique restrictions. One of these restrictions is that they are not able to choose where they live. While they can make requests, parole agents or the parole board generally make the decision based on a complicated set of factors including a man's gang affiliation, the nature of his crime, and the stability of the available households. Where a parolee lives is important in determining how able he is to see his children. Research suggests, not surprisingly, that fathers who live close to their children see them more often than fathers who live far away (McKenry et al. 1992; Teachman 1991). In a study of young fathers, Lerman (1993) found that while a quarter of young fathers lived more than one hundred miles from their children, these men accounted for 52 percent of those who did not have contact with their children.

Among the paroled fathers in the survey, about 25 percent reported that they lived in a different town from their children. For some of these men, this was not a change from their housing situation prior to their incarceration. Other men, however, lived near their children before being incarcerated and were either paroled to a new town or were paroled to their old town but their children had moved. Although I do not have direct evidence for this, the parolees' inability to live where they chose likely resulted in two contradictory outcomes for child visitation. Some men probably saw their children less than they would have liked because they lived far away and had little access to a car. At the same time, some men might have preferred to be paroled farther from their children because the children's proximity resulted in more pressure to see them. As expected, the paroled fathers who lived in the same town as their children saw those children, on average, a point and a half (on a 6-point scale) more than those men who lived in a different town from their children.

Knowing how often paroled fathers see their children is important, but it does not tell us what happens between the men and their children during visits. It is possible that men simply watch their children play and do not really interact with them. On the other hand, it is possible that they interact intensively with their children and take an active part in caring for them. To gain insight about this question, I asked survey respondents how often they were alone with their children. It turns out that a substantial minority did not see their children alone; they only saw them when their child's mother or their own mother was present. These other adults served as the primary caretaker while the father "visited" his child. Of those young men who had seen their child in the previous month, about 30 percent told me they had not been alone with the child at all. Of the 70 percent of fathers who had been alone with their children, most reported that they had done so only a few times.

I asked the fathers about the different activities they engaged in with their children when they visited. Their responses suggested that the most common way they interacted was through play. Excluding those men who had not seen their children, 65 percent reported that they played with their children at least once in the previous month. About 61 percent said they had taken their children out to the park or the zoo. A significantly smaller percentage told me that they engaged in some of the routine tasks associated with child rearing. For example, of the young men whose children were still in diapers, 50 percent said that they had not changed their child's diaper at all in the previous month. Most of those who had changed a diaper had done so five or fewer times in the previous month.

The fact that the nonresident fathers reported that they spent less time on child care and child rearing tasks than they did in play confirmed my impressions from the parenting class. Most of the stories that class participants told about their kids involved playing games. When there were discussions about whose responsibility it was to change diapers and handle child care, most of the young men said that, while they thought men should participate, they themselves were not very involved. It does not appear the paroled fathers are unusual in this respect. In a study of white and black parents of third and fourth graders, Annette Lareau (2000) found that fathers were "an important source of entertainment" for children but did not participate equally in "daily custodial care." There is little evidence to suggest that there are racial/ethnic differences. In a review of the literature, Mirandé (1991) found that the majority of studies reveal only minor differences between racial/ethnic groups. Those differences which were found did not support the idea that any group's methods of fathering were inferior. All three groups interacted in ways that were "warm, nurturing, and companionable" toward their children. Among paroled fathers, this appears to be the case as well. While I was not able to witness men's interaction with their children directly, I did ask them about the activities they engage in when they see their children. There were not significant differences between the racial/ethnic groups on any of these measures—from reading books, to taking children to the playground, to watching movies with them. Black, white, and Latino men appear to be engaging in the same activities with children, just not at the same rate.

In this chapter, I have discussed the quality and type of relationships paroled men build with their children. In the next, I step back from a direct examination of the father/child relationship to explore the men's larger social world. How does a man's relationship with key people, including his friends, family, and mother of his child, provide a context within which he makes decisions about spending time with children? It becomes clear that to understand the father/child relationship, we must consider the role of a wide range of other people in encouraging and discouraging a man's involvement.

4

Negotiating Relationships

Of the 258 surveys conducted for this project, the most challenging to schedule was with a young man named Adam. He had two jobs and five children, so I expected it to be difficult to find a time to meet with him. What surprised me, however, was that the scheduling problems we encountered had little to do with either his jobs or his children. Instead, it quickly became apparent that making an appointment with Adam required negotiation with several members of his family. The problems began when his wife convinced herself that I was calling to arrange a romantic rendezvous with him. Once this misunderstanding was cleared up, I had to negotiate with both Adam's wife and his mother to find a time when he did not have obligations to either of them. Although this specific situation was extreme, it was not unusual. A paroled father's daily activity schedule, including involvement with his children, is frequently determined by his relationships with other people. In this chapter, I explore how a man's relationships with his mother, his girlfriend, his friends, the mother of his children, her boyfriend, and her family all influence his involvement with his children. I also discuss the impact of prison and parole on these relationships.

Children's Mothers

Not surprisingly, the person who usually wields the most influence in a man's decisions about child involvement is the mother of his children. In the survey, I asked the men to tell me the primary factor determining how much contact they have with their children. Twenty-three percent of the nonresident fathers cited their relationship with the child's mother. The in-depth interviews yielded similar findings.

The literature on fatherhood suggests two important reasons why mothers play such an important role in determining a young father's contact with his children. First, most mothers live with their children and act as a "gatekeeper" to control any interaction between them and their fathers. They regulate the time, frequency, and duration of visits (Seltzer and Brandreth 1994). When couples are not getting along, or when a mother feels the man is not living up to his commitments, she is able to restrict his access to the child. Just over half of the nonresident paroled fathers reported that they had been denied visitation at least once.

Frank Furstenberg (1995) identifies a second way in which the relationship between men and their children's mother affects father/child contact. In his work with young parents, he finds that men do not view their relationship with their children as separate from their relationship with the children's mother. Men see mothers and children as a "package deal." When the bond between a man and his child's mother weakens, or is weak to begin with, the father separates himself from both the mother and the child. Furstenberg points out that weak parental relationships are particularly common among adolescents. Young couples often do not know each other well before they have a child and, in some cases, are "virtual strangers." This observation is certainly true for the paroled fathers. As described in chapter 1, most had known their partners for less than six months before the woman became pregnant.

Exacerbating the problems caused by brief courtships, research suggests that teenage relationships may take place in an atmosphere of hostility and antagonism between the sexes. Elijah Anderson's work (1990) with young men in an urban neighborhood, for example, suggests that relationships between men and women can be likened to a game where both sides are trying to achieve their goal. The game is essentially futile, however, because both teams are striving for different goals: men for sex and women for love, affection, and marriage. Anderson finds that, as a result, relations between the sexes are strained, distrustful, and manipulative. His findings are confirmed by other researchers. William J. Wilson (1996), for example, calls relationships between black inner-city men and women "often fractious and antagonistic."

From Wilson and Anderson's findings it would be easy to conclude that gender relations in poor, primarily black, urban areas are unique. In truth, however, poverty may simply intensify problematic gender relations that exist in the larger culture. Terry Arendell (1995) conducted a study with adult divorced men and found that they tended to be hostile toward their ex-partners and toward women in general. In her interviews with the men, derogatory comments toward women and toward ex-wives were "commonplace." The men Arendell studied were very different from the men Anderson and Wilson studied—they were middle-aged and middle-class—but their responses toward women were remarkably similar. A study done by Schuldberg and Guisinger (1991) with a different sample of middle- and upper-class divorced men came to similar conclusions about antagonism toward women.

Like the divorced men in Arendell's study and the men with whom Anderson and Wilson worked, the paroled fathers perceived deep divisions between themselves and women. Notably, I found that mistrust and antagonism were present among men of all three racial and ethnic backgrounds. On the survey I asked young men if they agreed with the statement "Many teenage girls who get pregnant do so to try and trap their boyfriends." About 70 percent agreed with the statement, and there were no significant differences by race/ethnicity.

I observed in parenting class that the paroled fathers have something of a "siege mentality" in their dealings with women. They believe that women take a perverse pleasure in causing them trouble. One particularly memorable illustration of this attitude occurred when we were discussing domestic violence. The teacher, John, was trying to convince the parolees that they should not hit women. What follows is an excerpt from my field notes.

> John talked at length about how men should not hit women. At some point Caleb brought up abusive women. This really seemed to be a major concern of most of the guys. Caleb wanted to know what to do if a woman was being verbally or emotionally abusive toward him. John first tried to say that this class was about men—the women weren't there—but the students kept pushing him to talk about it. John finally asked how many couples they knew where the woman was abusive to the man. Caleb couldn't think of any, and neither could anyone else offhand, but they all agreed that it was common.

This theme of abusive or manipulative women came up again and again throughout the parenting class. A reading of the literature on young and poor mothers reveals that women level strikingly similar accusations against men. Edin's work with women on welfare (2000), for example, gives a particularly bleak picture of women's attitudes. Her respondents reported hostility and distrust of men caused by experiences ranging from infidelity to domestic violence to abdication of responsibility for children. While men and women disagree about who is at fault, both groups acknowledge the existence of serious antagonism between the genders.

Intergender hostility contributes to relationship problems between young parents and makes it difficult for them to maintain romantic relationships with each other. Given this, it is not surprising that the paroled fathers reported that their relationships with the mothers of their children were of very short duration. Of the couples who were dating at the time of their child's conception, 17 percent had broken up before the birth. About 39 percent of the men in the survey reported that they were no longer dating the mother of their oldest child, and of the forty-five men with children aged five or older, only four were still romantically involved with the mothers.

While relationship breakups were common among men of all racial/ethnic backgrounds, the Latino fathers were less likely to break up than either whites or blacks. Over 45 percent of the Latino men were still romantically involved with the mothers of their children, while this was true for only 39 percent of whites and 21 percent of blacks.[1] Mercer Sullivan's comparative work in black and Latino urban neighborhoods (1993) provides insight into why this might be the case. He found that there was a great deal of family and community pressure on young Latino parents to work out any difficulties and to remain a couple. As a result, young fathers were more likely to stay in relationships and to marry the mothers of their children. Regardless of the reason, the fact that Latino paroled fathers are somewhat more likely to maintain relationships with children's mothers probably helps explain why they are more involved with their children than are whites.

Conflict and relationship stability between parents may affect a father's interaction with his children. First, the quality of parental relationships is the primary determinant of whether or not men live with their children. Conflict can cause the relationship between parents who live together to disintegrate, thereby causing the father to move to a new residence. Not surprisingly, nonresident fathers are less involved with their children than are resident fathers.[2] Parental conflict also appears to affect the quality of interaction men have with their children. Lamb and Elster's work with fathers (1986), ages sixteen to twenty-nine, and their six-month-old children indicates that the quality of the young men's interaction with their babies is significantly and positively correlated with the quality of the mother/father interaction. These findings are similar to those from studies conducted with adult fathers and their children (Belsky et al. 1991; Brody, Pillegrini, and Sigel 1986).

Impact of the Prison on Relationships with Mothers

While it is clear that the paroled fathers believe there are deep divisions between themselves and the women in their lives, one should not take this to mean that parolees are necessarily different from other economically disadvantaged young men. Anderson and Wilson's work suggests that, in terms of antagonism between the sexes, paroled fathers are much like their nonparoled peers. My interactions with the parolees, however, indicate that they face unique pressures in their relationship with their children's mother.

One of the first problems newly released men encounter is that the mothers of their children frequently have changed. This makes it hard for the men to reestablish the relationship. After two years in prison, Doug complained, "Now that I'm home, our relationship is not as good as it was before I went to jail. It's like we are trying to get to know each other again. 'Cause over the years people change, you know. You come home and they are not the same. It's kind of like meeting a new person again. It's hard."

When asked how twenty-six months of incarceration affected the relationship he had with the mother of his child, Tyrell commented: "It was like we wasn't really close friends anymore. It was like we didn't really know each other 'cause I was gone longer than I was with her. You know, so we had only been together maybe a year and a half, two years and then I got locked up for over two years."

The literature on spouses of prison inmates suggests that the primary way in which women change during their partner's incarceration is that they become much more independent and self-sufficient. When the men return, the women do not want to go back to playing the submissive role (Hunter 1986; McCubin et al. 1975; McDermott and King 1992). This new independence is hard for many men to accept, especially when they have spent their time in jail imagining how their wife or girlfriend used to act. This theme appeared in my interviews with the paroled fathers. I asked Hernaldo how the mother of his child had reacted when he was released from prison:

> She was happy at the time, but as the days went by you could see that . . . 'cause when I was gone she always used to party, doing this, going out. I wanted to be tied down with her and the kids, get to know each other again. She wasn't ready for it, I guess, 'cause she was used to that whole time that I was away just partying and doing whatever.

As time went by, Hernaldo was unable to reconcile his image of what his child's mother used to be with the person she had become. Eventually they broke up. Paroled juvenile fathers are not the only group to have difficulty with the transition back into relationships with wives and girlfriends. In a seven-year study of 241 prisoners of war and their families, for example, Edna Hunter (1986) found that returning POWs had a higher rate of divorce than did a matched control group of military families (30 percent as compared with 12 percent). Kathleen McDermott and Roy King's (1992) research with newly released adult prisoners in Britain indicates that they experience high levels of stress in their relations with wives and children. A primary reason for this is that the children and women have undergone many changes in the men's absence. As a result, the men are no longer able to occupy their former role and find themselves not knowing how to act around their family.

Another relationship challenge newly released men face is that their parole status gives women more control over them, dramatically altering the balance of power. The mothers are aware that parolees can be returned to the institution for any violation of their parole, and they understand that if they report a violation it is likely that the man will be arrested. This problem was discussed in one of the first parenting classes I attended. The theme of the class was domestic violence, and during the break a very bright young man named Jacob nervously approached the teacher. Jacob told him that he was trying hard not to hit his girlfriend but felt that she was always provoking him and then threatening to call his parole agent. He said he was at a loss how to handle the situation. Echoing similar sentiments, Charles told me,

> Two years ago, when my daughter was born and we split up, it was hard. We went through a lot because, after she had the baby, she had an attitude I didn't know she had. So then she started jeopardizing my parole, calling my officer, telling my parole officer lies and stuff. So I had to just cut her off, because my freedom I felt was more important at the time.

The threat of being returned to the institution is obviously very serious, and men will go to great lengths to avoid it. Jeremy, a father of two, told me that he took custody of his elder son when the child's mother was arrested. He was concerned for the boy's welfare and did not want him to go back to the mother when she was released.

> And then she got out, probably a week and a half later, and she called my grandma's house . . . talking about bringing my son home. . . . "If you don't bring my son home, I'm going to call the police on you." Then my grandma's like, "Go ahead and take him home, take him home. You don't need more trouble. You're already on parole. Just take him home."

These comments indicate that mothers of children can use the parole system to exert power over men and limit the access they have to their children.

Compounding the relationship difficulties that newly released men face is the weight of unmet promises many have made to their children's mother from prison. As discussed in chapters 2 and 3, men spend time in prison building up expectations for their own behavior after they are released. Once they develop this set of expectations, they naturally share their hopes with their children and with their children's mother. By the time they are released, the high expectations they have for themselves are also shared by mothers and children. Marco described the promises he made to the mother of his child while he was in the institution.

> Like people always talk, you always write this and that to your girl-friend, "When I get out, it's going to be like this, like that." This and that, and this and that. And you get out and it's like, "You wrote it. Do it. Come on, I'm waiting for it, you know."

Many incarcerated men tell their hopes and plans to the mother of their children because they are excited and want to share them. Some also use their plans to encourage these women to stay in a romantic relationship with them. By making promises about how they will change, they raise the hopes of the mother. Tony described how he had kept his relationship with the mother of his child together by building up her expectations:

> I saw a lot [of breakups in prison], but for me, we got closer. The bad
> part was we got closer because of what I was telling her were lies. You
> know, I was telling her I was going to change when I get out, because I
> didn't want to be here. And I actually went home, and it was all a bunch
> of lies.

Mothers adopt the expectations the young men create and then begin to embellish them. Sam told me that he got angry because the
mother of his child had such high expectations for him. "She
wanted to see what I was really made of. At times, she made me
angry . . . 'cause she talked about how good it was going to be and
I did, too." When young men are finally released, they are under
great pressure to live up to the promises they have made.

As they fail to live up to their own high expectations, they and
their children's mother become disillusioned and disappointed.
Sam described what happened with the mother of his child when
he was finally released:

> And when I got my job I was trying real hard to succeed and make ev-
> erything right, as good as I could, 'cause she was talking about not show-
> ing her nothing, I'm still the same person I was before I got locked up.
> And that really made me feel bad, you know what I'm saying? It down-
> graded me.

Marco, like Sam, found that he could not live up to his girlfriend's
expectations. He returned home from prison and was allowed to
live with her and his child. Things quickly soured, however, and
the girlfriend began complaining that he was a failure. "I got out
and I tried. I got a job. I was making a little bit of money and I
tried. . . . But then after a while I think it just gets back into the
same routine. You know, you get tired and you just work your way
back into that same old crap."

There are many ways in which paroled men can fail to live up to a mother's expectations, but perhaps the most damaging is when they are sent back to prison. Parolees can be returned to prison either because they commit a new crime or because they violate the conditions of their parole. Parole violations range from drug use to association with former gang associates or failure to report for meetings with a parole agent. In 1996, about 16 percent of the men in California Youth Authority institutions were there on parole violations (CYA 1996). Because one of the primary promises men make to their children and their children's mothers is that they will not go back to prison, their arrest destroys any trust they may have been able to build since returning home.

New Partners of Both Parents

The strains inherent in adolescent relationships, coupled with the unique pressures of parole, ensure that most of the romantic relationships between paroled men and the mothers of their children come to an end. When this happens, both partners are free to date. Among the paroled fathers, 30 percent reported that they were dating someone new, and 32 percent reported that their children's mother had a new boyfriend; 18 percent said they did not know the dating status of the mother. Given that Latino fathers tend to stay in romantic relationships with children's mothers longer than whites or blacks, it is not surprising that they are less likely to be dating someone new. At the time of the survey, about 42 percent of the white parolees were dating someone new as compared with 39 percent for blacks and 23 percent for Latinos. Similarly, a smaller percentage of Latinos reported that their children's mothers were dating someone new (28 percent as compared with 36 percent for blacks and 42 percent for whites).

My interviews with the paroled fathers suggest that new partners for either the mother or the father can play a key role in determining a man's involvement with his children. A number of men talked about how they began to see less of their children when the mother began dating someone new. John, the father of a three-year-old, reported that he did not like going to see his son when the mother's new boyfriend was around.

> I don't really be feeling comfortable because, you know, I feel that he doesn't like me—the fact that I come over but he don't come out and say that and then I just be feeling like I know that's really the way he feels but he not saying it, so that to me feels funny when I know a person is feeling one way and acting another—that makes me feel uncomfortable. I just don't like to be around a situation like that.

Rodney described a similar situation:

> Like right now, you know, the person that her mom's with, I think he detects that there's still something going on, or that something might happen between us. I don't understand why he thinks that, but it's wrong. She's with him, and I'm with who I'm with, and we both getting on. We living two separate lives. And I don't know why he thinks that but for one minute I didn't see her for a while because I had the phone number and everything and she was staying at one apartment and she moved and she didn't inform me or nothing about moving, changing phone numbers. Didn't tell me nothing. Really it was because of him. It wasn't really her. It was him telling her to do that.

A young father's contact with a mother's new boyfriend is often fraught with the kind of tension John and Rodney described. It appears that there are at least three forms this tension can take: the father not getting along with the new boyfriend; being jealous of him; or feeling threatened by him. Sometimes, however, it is not the father who chooses to reduce contact with the children. In the survey, almost half of the young men whose child's mother was dating someone else agreed with the statement "Her boyfriend or husband doesn't like you or is jealous of you and he doesn't want you coming around to see your child very often."

Furstenberg's work (1995) suggests one reason why men's contact with children decreases when mothers find new boyfriends. He explains that a mother who begins a serious new relationship often involves this partner with her children. If the new partner becomes central to the child's life, the father may feel that he has been replaced. The father may also feel ashamed that his level of involvement does not match that of the new boyfriend. The feelings of guilt, jealousy, and shame may drive men from active participation with their children. Stack's (1974) work in a poor black community confirms the link between new boyfriends and decreased father/child contact. Her data indicate that there is often hostility between the father and the new man that causes the father to withdraw from his children.

Among the paroled fathers, jealousy and animosity do not appear to be limited to the relationship between the father and the mother's new boyfriend. The in-depth interviewees reported that their relationship with a new girlfriend sometimes resulted in similar problems. What follows is an excerpt from an interview with Robert, a young man who sees his child sporadically because of hostility between his child's mother and his new girlfriend:

> Robert: And then she started talking about my girlfriend. "Oh, you can't come over here. You can't see the baby unless you leave her. Don't bring her over here, or I won't let you see the baby," and this type of stuff.
>
> A.N.: So what did you do?
>
> Robert: You know, try to work the best way I could. Lie to her and tell her, yeah, okay, she's gone, whatever, so I could see my son. But she found out, [and] she disappeared. And then you know this all went on in three months and then I got locked up.

Like Robert, Hernaldo had little contact with his son. He told me that the mother of his child began to withhold visitation when he started to date another woman. When I asked him why, he said, "She's just the jealous type, you know. 'Cause the other girl I'm with now that I have two kids by, she's jealous, she don't like her. I guess she carries a grudge about that." Michael told me that his son's mother continued to let him see his child while he was dating a new girlfriend, but when he married the girlfriend, the mother suddenly began to limit his visits.

> A.N.: How does your wife get along with your son's mother?
> Michael: Well, they don't get along. I mean, they never really bumped heads with each other. They know each other. She know I got a new daughter by her, and I've got a son by her. So I think [when] my son's mom found out I got married, it really hit her, so that probably did something, too.

The responses I received from both interview and survey respondents suggest that the kind of conflict and antagonism these men have witnessed between their child's mother and their new girlfriend is quite common. I asked survey respondents who had a new girlfriend to rate on a scale from 0 to 5 how well their child's mother got along with their new girlfriend. The distribution was heavily weighted to the low end with 44 percent ranking their relationship as a 0 (extremely poor), and only 18 percent reporting that their relationship was a 4 or 5.

Impact of the Prison on New Partner Relationships

In the last chapter, I described the emotional distress many men feel when they return home from prison to find another man acting as "daddy" for their children. While most of the men who told me about this expressed some degree of jealousy or anger, those who had been replaced by the boyfriend or husband of the child's mother reported particularly strong emotions. Marco described what happened when he got out of prison and went to see the mother of his children:

> I got out and I didn't know. Just that day I found out she was with somebody else. So I was like, cool, I just want to see my kids. I saw my kids, and told him, "Hey, whatever, you know, I ain't with her no more. You are. . . . Come here. [He gestures like he gestured to the new boyfriend.] Don't ever touch my kids. I'll break your hands. Don't ever try to get a hand on 'em, you know. Those are my kids."

Marco's vehement anger mirrored the reactions of other men whose children's mother had started dating while they were in prison. One of the reasons their anger was so intense was that most had been given the "summer shake" in prison to free the mother to date the new boyfriend. To return home and find the same man playing "daddy" to their children was extremely difficult to accept. Randy was one of the men who fit this description. In response to a question about how incarceration changed his relationship with the mother of his child he told me the following:

> Randy: We were together before I went in and were not together when I came out. So that's how it changed, and then we come apart. I guess it really depends on the relationship also. You know, if they can wait for you or not. But that's pretty rare.
>
> A.N.: And what happened in your case?
>
> Randy: She met somebody else. Got pregnant with his kid. Had it.
>
> A.N.: What happened? Did she call you?
>
> Randy: She never called me. She just quit coming to see me. She would make excuses and she wouldn't call me, or she wouldn't be at my grandmother's house when she knew I was gonna call there, 'cause she didn't have a phone. She didn't write me letters. She just quit coming to see me. No letters, no replies, no nothing.

A.N.: So how did you find out what happened?

Randy: My son told me, and my grandmother told me and my mom. That's how I found out.

It is obvious that Randy was hurt when his child's mother broke up with him. He told me that he spent the remainder of his prison term thinking about just how upset he was. By the time he was released, he carried a great deal of anger, most of it directed toward the mother's new boyfriend.

Family Support

In his work with young black fathers, Anderson (1990) found that the men's families, especially their mothers, play a pivotal role in determining how much they see their children. These mothers often make the ultimate decision about the level of their son's responsibility toward his children—especially in cases where paternity is in doubt. The mother visits the newborn to determine whether or not her son is the father. If she decides that her son should take responsibility for a child, she encourages him to be involved. In addition, she often provides support and care for the child and enlists other family members to participate. By bringing the child into her family network, a man's mother actively solicits his involvement with the child.

While none of the paroled fathers directly attributed their level of contact with their children to the involvement of their mothers, there was ample evidence to support Anderson's findings. The paroled fathers who saw their children most frequently often talked about how their own mothers took an active hand in helping to raise them. Paul, who sees his two children daily, commented:

> My mom, she does everything. She takes my kid to every hospital appointment there is. She has them every day. She enrolls them in school,

you know. You see, my baby's mom, she thinks she got away with a lot of stuff, but every time we went to the doctor's, it was my mom who filled out the papers for them. At school it's the same thing.

Jose sees his daughter daily:

> She grew up with mostly my family, you know what I mean? They share her on weekends, weekdays, you know? My mom watches her, picks her up. We have no problem with that, you know what I mean, even though I'm not with her mother and all.

These quotes and others like them suggest that there is a link between grandmother and father involvement. Of course, the relationship is undoubtedly reciprocal: Involved grandmothers encourage a father's involvement, and involved fathers encourage the grandmother's involvement. In this mutually reinforcing situation, each encourages the other to higher levels of participation and commitment.

A man's mother is not the only family member who determines his level of involvement. A child's maternal family is also extremely important. During an in-depth interview, Frank gave several reasons why he rarely sees his son, including the hostility he encountered from his girlfriend's mother. Robert discussed the role his son's mother had in promoting the grandmother's negative attitude:

> She had her mom thinking I was the bad guy in the whole thing, and I wasn't going to try to be there. This child was going to be born, and I couldn't allow myself to stay in that situation for too long. Something bad would happen.

Like Robert, Miguel also felt disapproval from the parents of his child's mother. Both parents took an active role in preventing him from seeing the child.

> I felt weird going to her house 'cause her daddy said all kinds of trash and start cussing me out. I didn't blame her, man. I just felt kind of uncomfortable. But I wanted to . . . pick her [the daughter] up to take her out to go eat. That's the way I wanted it to be, you know. I liked it like that. I wanted her to spend days with me, but her [the mother's] mother wouldn't let me. She said, "I don't trust you." 'Cause she thought I was into all kinds of gangs and stuff.

Frank Furstenberg's work (1995) with fathers in the inner city can help us understand the comments of Frank and George. He finds that the expectations and behavior of the mother's family have a profound impact on the father. Families that expect a low level of involvement by the father transmit this feeling and help create a self-fulfilling situation. Young men are quite able to sense hostility from the mother's family, and this makes them less inclined to have contact with that family and, consequently, with their own children. At the same time, families who disapprove of the young father can serve in a gatekeeping capacity to prevent him from seeing his child (Allen and Doherty 1996). In his work in a black neighborhood, for example, Sullivan (1993) found that maternal grandmothers and other female kin sometimes try to limit an unemployed father's access to his children.

In general, it appears that family plays a role in encouraging or discouraging a father's involvement with his children. Research suggests, however, that there may be racial and ethnic variations in family support. Both black and Latino family structure have been found to be particularly conducive to the provision of support for children. Carol Stack, in a classic study published in 1974, explored how economically disadvantaged blacks use extensive kin networks to support children. While fathers might not be living with children, they link them to family networks that provide guidance as well as material support. Black families are not "fatherless" but rather are part of "cooperative domestic exchange." Recent work suggests that, although Stack may have painted an overly positive picture of the smooth functioning of kin networks, they still perform strongly in the black community (Cramer and McDonald 1996). Latino families, like black, also tend to have strong extended family networks. Most of the available research points to the loyalty family members have for each other. Latinos provide emotional and financial support (often referred to as "familism") for extended family in ways that other groups do not. The extended family has also been found to play a more important role for Mexican Americans than for other groups (Suarez-Orozco and Suarez-Orozco 1995; Walters and Chapman 1991).

The centrality of family support systems is apparent among the black and Latino paroled fathers. The children of the Latino parolees, for example, were more likely than either blacks or whites to live with their extended families. Half of the Latino children lived with their maternal grandparents, while this was true for only 25 percent of blacks and 39 percent of whites. Both blacks and Latinos were more likely than whites to report that their own mothers were involved with their children. I asked the paroled fathers how often their children saw their paternal grandmothers. On a 6-point scale of children's contact with the parolees' mothers, the average score was 2.00 for whites, 3.62 for Latinos, and 3.48 for blacks.[3] These differences are fairly striking and may help to explain why black and Latino fathers see their children more often than do whites.

Impact of the Prison on Family Relationships

Not surprisingly, it appears that prison places a strain on the relationship a man has with his child's maternal family. Families who were originally supportive of a young man being romantically involved with their daughter often changed their attitude after his arrest. For families who were not enthusiastic about the young man from the start, his arrest only seemed to strengthen their negative feelings. Miguel told me about how the disapproval of his child's maternal grandfather prevented him from seeing his child while he was in prison and after his release.

> Miguel: Yeah, her mother wanted to bring her [the daughter], but see, the problem was her father at first didn't want to let her bring her. My daughter's grandfather didn't want to let his daughter come. If his daughter couldn't come, my daughter couldn't come.
> A.N.: So why did he feel that way?
> Miguel: He said I was in here for something bad and I was irresponsible. You know, if I was in a place like this, obviously I'm no good and have no reason to see her.

Miguel's experience with his child's maternal family is fairly typical. Many of the paroled fathers returned home to find the maternal family less than enthusiastic about the prospect of their daughter or grandchild's involvement with them.

Friends

Attending parenting classes gave me many opportunities to watch the paroled fathers interact with one another. I was often surprised by how supportive they were, at least in terms of fatherhood issues. I particularly remember one night when a man said he was having difficulty getting his child to switch from bottles to cups. The other men proceeded to have an earnest and quite lengthy discussion about what he should do. I witnessed similar moments when men genuinely encouraged each other to take an active role in raising their children. Because the parenting classes were artificial situations, I wondered if this type of supportive behavior continued outside the classroom. It seemed quite possible that, on the streets, peer pressure to spend time with friends overshadowed support for time spent with children. My interactions with the paroled fathers suggest that both possibilities are true: Some friendships function to support and encourage child contact, others to discourage it. One key difference between the two appears to be whether a man's friends are active fathers themselves.

Paroled fathers whose friends were actively involved with their own children tended to give a much more favorable report on the amount of support they received. They felt that their friends understood their desire to spend time with their children and encouraged them to do so. One benefit to a man's friendships with other fathers is that the men are able to take their children places together. Paul, who sees his child several times a week, said:

> Yeah, like my best friend, I go over to his house when he has his son there. I can still be with him when he has his son. When I have my son, my friends will tell me, "Oh, let's go." If it's somewhere like Great America, they'll be all, "Let's go take them there," or something. They are all supportive when I need a ride somewhere with my son to go do something. A lot of them will come with me when I go do stuff, you know. We take our kids out.

I asked Randy, a father of two, how his friends felt about his having children.

> They understand. In fact, one of my best friends, he just got married, and his wife has a little boy, so he's taken on that responsibility. On top of that, he found out a week ago that she's pregnant. . . . Yeah, and one of the guys that I met when I was locked up was from [my town] also. And he has a little boy, and he ended up getting married about four months ago and he just had a little girl, so we're in the same boat. We ain't no party animals, go out and tear up the town or nothing. Every once in a while, go out for a minute, maybe two hours, come back and just watch movies and talk. It's about how wild we are.

These quotes, and many others like them, suggest that men who are actively involved with their own children can be a strong force in encouraging others to spend more time with their children. Childless friends, on the other hand, appear to exert pressure in the opposite direction. The paroled fathers who had few or no friends with children tended to complain about not receiving support for spending time with their children. Instead, they said that they felt pressure to spend time with their friends.

The literature on young fathers provides insight into the relationship between a father's friends and his involvement with his children. Anderson's work in an inner-city neighborhood (1990) as well as Teti and Lamb's 1986 study clearly support the importance of the peer group in determining fathering attitudes and behavior. Their research indicates that, in general, young male culture supports men who take care of their children. The young men in Anderson's study, for example, encouraged fathers to be involved with their children, and even taunted those who abdicated responsibility. At the same time, however, the peer group strongly discourages men from establishing monogamous relationships with women. In order to maintain their status in the peer group, young men must declare their independence from women and generally refuse to be "tied down" to anyone. It is likely that these peer group pressures work against each other. Men are encouraged by friends to see their children, but they run the risk of angering the mothers of their children by yielding to peer pressure and refusing to be monogamous.

My experience with the paroled fathers suggests that whether or not a man is involved with a gang influences his involvement with his children and adds another layer of complexity to the relationship between friendship and fathering behavior. Although some gangs may be quite supportive of a father's involvement with his children, the gang lifestyle is simply not compatible with responsible fatherhood The problem for gang members is that an active street life, combined with active fatherhood, can endanger their children. A few of the young men, all of them former or current gang members, talked about the difficulties of being with their children in their neighborhoods. Jose told me that he didn't take his daughter outside his house.

> I'm afraid for my daughter, you know what I mean? I ain't worried about myself, what they could do to me, the same thing I could do back. I mean, it's only flesh, you know what I mean? We're destined to die, that's the way I look at it. So however I'm going to die, I'm going to die. I can't avoid that, you know what I mean? So if they shoot me, stab me, whatever, they go both ways. If I die, somebody is going to do back to them, so I'm not really worried about myself. I could care less. But my daughter, my family, and everybody else that's around me, they have nothing to do with that. That's a different story.

Tony told me about the day he got out of prison:

> I was going to make up for lost time. I wanted him with me every minute, [but] that changed because the first day I was out actually I was running into people I didn't get along with and I thought I can't have him with me when I'm out on the streets because I wouldn't be able to live if something happened to him. After that first day we were on the streets together, but after that, when I'd go out, I went by myself. I didn't take him to public places. I was so scared of what happened if I got caught by somebody I didn't get along with, somebody I did something wrong to. How would they react if I'm here with my baby?

As these quotes illustrate, both Tony and Jose are distressed by their inability to go out with their children. From an outsider's perspective, the solution seems obvious: They should cut their gang ties. The truth, however, is that street life offers many benefits which are difficult to abandon. In response to a question about how prison had changed him, Tony commented:

> It made me different, not in a bad way. It made me different, like I wanted to spend more time with him [his son]. I wanted to be around him all the time. It's hard to explain, because I wanted to be around him all the time, but the street life was more exciting. I could go around the streets and act wild. I know I can always go home and he'll be waiting for me. So really, in my heart he was first priority; in my mind I subconsciously made him second priority because I chose the streets and spent all my time there.

Men who are drawn to the excitement of street or gang life find themselves in a no-win situation. They are fascinated by the streets and want to spend time there, but it is too dangerous for children. As a result, they can no longer risk taking their children out to public places like the park or the zoo. Staying at home seems dull, especially in comparison with the streets, and so begins a pattern of increased street time and decreased child time.

Impact of the Prison on Friendship

While many young people confront pressures from the streets, newly paroled men may be particularly susceptible. It appears that having been to the California Youth Authority enhances a man's status in the eyes of his friends and fellow gang members. The in-depth interview respondents told me that the people they knew seemed to admire and fear them more when they were released. Simply spending time in prison seems to have this effect, but especially admired on release are those young men who were adept at earning the other inmates' fear and respect while in prison. Stories of an incarcerated man's fighting prowess or toughness leak out of the institution and build a reputation on the streets. Paul, a young man from the suburbs, told me that he fought a lot in the institution. He described what he was like when he was first released:

> I had to hold up this image when I first got out because . . . I find I'm highly respected around here. . . . Then I got out and I was always running around. So when I got out, everyone was like, "Oh, you're crazy," you know, for this or that. And I never noticed it 'til my friend woke me up to it and told me, "You been trying to hold up an image for a long time," and you know, I was like, "What are you talking about?" He said, "Because you was known to get out of YA and you were known to fight and do this and that," and I was like, "Yeah, that's true," and I barely realized it, but it took me a long time. I'd been out almost two years, and I barely noticed that. I was trying to hold up an image all the time.

Men who are paroled back into their own neighborhoods often discover that they have higher status, and the streets become a place where they are validated and can feel good about themselves. Such attention is especially difficult to shun when the men fail to win respect and attention from their children.

In the beginning of this chapter, I discussed the difficulties I encountered while scheduling interview appointments with Adam and the other paroled fathers. It became clear that each of the fathers was enmeshed in a complex web of relationships that helped to determine his daily schedule. As this chapter illustrates, the influence of a man's relationships—with his children's mothers, friends, and family—extends well beyond appointment scheduling to directly impact involvement with his children. Mothers and other key people have the power to prevent the men from having contact with their children. More often, however, they simply encourage or discourage a man's involvement through their reactions to him. A father's incarceration puts strain on all of his relationships, and

it makes his active involvement in his children's lives more difficult.

The findings about young fatherhood and incarceration presented in this and previous chapters raise significant policy questions. How can we encourage men's involvement with their children? How can we mitigate the effects of incarceration and parole
on men's relationships with children? Can the structure of the
prison be changed to facilitate men's active participation in their
children's lives? Would such changes be desirable? I address these
and other policy questions in the next chapter.

5

Young Fatherhood, Incarceration, and Public Policy

The juvenile correctional system began in 1825 in New York with the creation of the first reform school. Before that time, juveniles who committed serious crimes were housed alongside adults in local jails. In many cases, judges pardoned children rather than send them to jail because they feared harm would come to them. These judges, however, were increasingly criticized for this practice. The public clearly favored punishment for criminal children. From the perspective of both the judges and the public, the opening of juvenile reform schools was an ideal solution. By the 1870s, there were more than fifty in operation (Schlossman 1995). Since then, the juvenile justice system has grown exponentially, and today it bears only a slight resemblance to the original reform-school system. To understand how we have evolved to the current system and where we should go from here, it is useful to briefly place the juvenile prison in its social and political context.

Since the early days of the reform schools, the public has vacillated between a desire to use the juvenile justice system to rehabilitate criminal youth and a desire to use it to punish. In *The Cycle of Juvenile Justice* (1992), Thomas Bernard illustrates how public opinion about the purpose of the prison cycles from punitive to rehabilitative. A cycle begins when public fears about crime intensify. Policymakers and prison officials respond to this public fear and implement restrictive and punitive policies in the prisons. At a certain point, however, concern arises over prison conditions, and reform efforts and rehabilitative programs are put into place. The cycle returns to punitive policies when the public realizes that there is still a high level of crime. As their fear again mounts, they place blame for crime on the "lenient" rehabilitative policies and insist that they be abandoned (Bernard 1992). Many of the changes in juvenile justice policies over time can be attributed to this punitive/rehabilitative cycle.

A second debate that has shaped the juvenile correctional system involves the presumed nature of children and adolescents. Central to the creation of the reform school was the idea that children were morally and behaviorally different from adults. Children were believed to be less culpable and more malleable than adults and were therefore seen as more receptive to rehabilitation efforts. This belief has persisted and has ensured that the juvenile correctional system remains separate from the adult system. It has also meant that the juvenile system is more geared toward rehabilitation than is the adult system, even during punitive periods. This is not to say, however, that opinions about the nature of children and adults remain static. The degree to which the two groups are seen as different has changed over time, and the juvenile correctional system has changed with it. At times when young people are viewed as being substantially different from adults, the two prison systems become distinct. In contrast, when juvenile offenders are seen as similar to adults, the systems more closely resemble each other (Scott and Grisso 1997).

As societal ideas have shifted about the purpose of prison and the nature of young people, changes have been made to the structure of the juvenile correctional system. In the early nineteenth century, public sentiment about the purpose of the prison tended toward rehabilitation. The early reform schools, therefore, were based on the idea that criminal children were wayward and needed guidance and rehabilitation. Reform schools stressed order and hard work so that young people could be taught deference and self-discipline. To this end, residents of the reform schools were given jobs and required to attend school. Significantly, the reform schools were not intended for the exclusive use of criminals; they also housed poor and immigrant children, who were seen as being in need of guidance (Schlossman 1995). The rehabilitative drive of this period corresponds with a societal view of children as essentially different from adults (Scott and Grisso 1997).

By the late 1800s, when prison overcrowding became widespread, many of the rehabilitative goals of the juvenile prisons were abandoned. The juvenile prisons began to adopt a much more punitive tone and to resemble adult prisons. By the end of the century, however, another cycle of rehabilitation began as reformers took note of the abysmal conditions in the reform schools. They discovered that inmates were mistreated and not taught the necessary skills to return to life in the community. By 1899, reformers had established juvenile courts and probation departments for adolescents. These efforts, once again, emphasized the desire to rehabilitate criminal youth. A third cycle of reform began in 1960 with the expansion of juvenile rights, the extension of psychological assessment and treatment, and new research suggesting that community-based treatment was effective (Bernard 1992; Schlossman 1995).

As with previous cycles of reform, the rehabilitative zeal of the 1960s eventually faded, and by the 1980s the public had begun demanding the implementation of punitive policies at juvenile prisons. This attitude still prevails, and there are numerous examples of the public desire to punish juvenile offenders. Pressure from the public, for example, has encouraged state legislatures to increase the sentence length for juvenile offenders while reducing their privileges. In California, legislators defined their new "Three Strikes" law to include crimes committed by juveniles who are sixteen or older. At the federal level, in 1997, the U.S. House of Representatives passed a bill authorizing the distribution of $1.6 billion to states that toughen penalties for juvenile offenders. As these examples make clear, fear about crime and a desire to punish criminals created an environment where increasing sentences is seen as the best way to prevent crime.

Corresponding to our more punitive attitude toward juvenile criminals, we have begun to view youthful offenders as similar to their adult counterparts. Increasingly, we do not make a distinction between children and adults when it comes to criminal acts. Children are seen as equally responsible for their actions as adults. This punitive mentality holds that any serious crime must be punished without regard to the age of the offender (Scott and Grisso 1997). Forty-five states passed laws during the 1990s making it easier to transfer juveniles to adult court.

The current correctional system is not a result of research and central planning. Instead, it is a complicated blend of sometimes conflicting ideas about the nature of youth and the purpose of the prison. The fact that there is a large and growing population of fathers in prison does little to influence prison structure. Until recently, information about the fatherhood status of inmates was not even part of prison records. This lack of interest in incarcerated fathers is in contrast to a significant interest in identifying incarcerated mothers. Motherhood has long been recognized and incorporated into prison structure. This can be seen in policies granting more lenient sentences to mothers because of their responsibility for dependents (Daly 1987). It can also be seen in policies within the prison. There are pilot programs operating in several states that allow women to live with infants in prison or to have more frequent visits with their children. Such programs simply do not exist for men.

Thinking Ahead: Public Policy for Paroled and Incarcerated Fathers

There are no easy solutions to the problems presented by incarcerated juvenile fathers. The topic is complex, politically volatile, and emotionally charged. It is difficult to find agreement on policies regarding the separate issues of young fatherhood and juvenile delinquency; when the two are combined, confusion and conflict result. People who support encouraging a father's active involvement with his children often revise their views when they realize that many young fathers have committed serious crimes. At the same time, people who generally favor harsh punishment for criminals suddenly modify their stance when they consider the fact that many juvenile delinquents are fathers. The complexity and emotional nature of these issues make it clear that public policy formulation presents many challenges.

As a starting point for policy discussion, it is important to acknowledge the immense social costs associated with incarcerating large numbers of young fathers. I have argued throughout this book that these costs are paid not only by incarcerated fathers but by their families and communities as well. This suggests that one of the primary goals of public policy should be to reduce levels of incarceration among fathers. I discuss here several specific policies that might help to accomplish this goal. First, we should expand educational and employment opportunities for young people, especially for those from impoverished communities. William J. Wilson's work (1996) shows that the flight of unskilled jobs from the inner city has resulted in decreased employment opportunities for young men, particularly for men of color. As described, there is evidence to suggest that criminal behavior can, in some cases, be reduced by the creation of strong employment and school ties in young men's lives (Sampson and Laub 1993).

Another strategy for reducing the number of fathers in prison is to reconsider the current trend toward lengthening juvenile sentences. As adult sentencing laws such as "Three Strikes" are increasingly applied to juveniles, young fathers will serve longer prison terms. By arbitrarily increasing the sentences for offenders, we lose potentially productive citizens and fathers to the correctional system. We need to reassess our sentencing policies to protect the public while limiting the amount of time served by juveniles. We should also investigate and employ alternatives to incarceration, including intensive probation, halfway houses, and electronic monitoring.

Placing limits on juvenile sentences will grant fathers more years with their growing children. Shortened sentences may also help reduce young men's "hard-timing" response (see chapter 2 for a discussion of hard timing as a coping response to the prison environment), thereby facilitating an increase in father/child contact during time in prison. Knowing they will be released in a reasonable amount of time can be a source of hope and a motivation to maintain outside relationships. Hard timing may also be reduced by the less crowded conditions made possible by a policy of shorter sentences. In 1987, 36 percent of juvenile correctional facilities exceeded capacity. By 1991 the corresponding figure was 47 percent. Research indicates that overcrowding is linked to higher levels of violence among inmates—against both other inmates and staff (Parent et al. 1994). While this type of problem has always been present in juvenile prisons, it has reached new levels. The increased stress on inmates may encourage them to reduce contact with children as they use "hard timing" as a strategy. Overcrowding and its attendant violence also forces prison staff to rely more heavily on punitive methods of achieving control—reinforcing the idea among inmates that punishment is an appropriate behavior modification technique.

While I believe that limits on juvenile sentencing could be beneficial, the political reality makes it clear that young fathers will continue to enter our correctional system. For this reason, it is imperative that we develop enlightened policies for dealing with them. In this chapter, I draw on the previous three to make policy recommendations. These recommendations are divided into two sections: one designed for incarcerated men and the other for men in the community, both those who have been to prison and those who have not. While these recommendations are far from complete, they provide a starting point for discussion.

Recommended Policies within the Prison

Provide Parenting Classes

During the in-depth interviews, many of the parolees talked enthusiastically about parenting classes they had taken while in prison or on parole. Their comments surprised me because I did not specifically ask about these classes. Instead, the parolees mentioned the classes in other contexts. For example, when asked how the YA could help fathers in prisons, Robert said,

> Just keep giving them information. Keep having those parenting classes, you know what I mean? Because all the information they give helps somebody, because it all pertains to a certain different situation somebody is going through. That's it there. Just keep giving them info. For the guys that have kids, they should make it mandatory that they go to a parenting class.

Robert is not unusual. Many of the parolees believed that parenting classes gave them valuable skills and knowledge. Because of the positive reactions of these men, I believe that such classes should be made more widely available to all incarcerated young fathers.

The parenting classes need to include several important features. First, information about birth control should be included in all classes. In the survey, I asked the men if they were using birth control regularly when their partner got pregnant. Over 65 percent said that they never used birth control. At the same time, over 85 percent said that they were not trying to get their partner pregnant when she conceived their oldest child. My observations suggest that there are several reasons the paroled fathers fail to use birth control. First, some felt that it was not "polite" to use birth control when romantically involved with the woman. The following excerpt from my field notes is one of several examples I can use to illustrate this point. The notes were taken in a class focusing on birth control. The teacher is Alexander:

> Alexander asks how many of us use condoms. Four of the parolees say they do. Alexander asks why those of us who don't use them don't. Arthur says that he doesn't because he's married. Somebody else says that they don't because they are only sleeping with one person. Arthur cuts in and says that you only use condoms with "Sanchas." Alexander asks him to repeat himself and then, still not understanding, he asks him to explain. The young Latino man to my right is laughing, as is another Latino in the room. Arthur seems a little embarrassed and glances at me. He says, "You know, like with a side thing—a side kick." Alexander says, "You mean with a one-night stand?" Arthur says yes, he only uses condoms then.

Men are willing to use condoms with "Sanchas" because they fear sexually transmitted diseases. Equally important, however, is their fear that the women might become pregnant. A successful sexual conquest of a "bad girl" may be a notch in a young man's belt, but having a child with one is not.

Another reason paroled fathers fail to use birth control is that they lack knowledge or have serious misconceptions about side effects. At least three men in separate parenting classes said that birth control pills always make women's hair fall out. Other men swore that birth control pills were linked to cancer. By receiving greater access to information, young men will have another tool to help them postpone childbearing. When birth control methods are taught in California Youth Authority parenting classes, the participants tend to be extremely interested and engaged. They clearly want to learn about contraception, and they want to postpone having more children.

Another important goal of parenting classes should be to provide the men with practical skills relating to basic child care. This is critical for young men who have little or no experience with children. Teaching them how to change diapers and what to do when a child is sick increases the ease with which these men can then interact with their families. Child development information should be included in the curriculum for all parenting classes. All parents worry that their children are not "normal." Presenting material about normal childhood development eases their concerns and helps them work with their children on age-appropriate skills.

Prison parenting classes have the potential to help inmates develop realistic expectations for how their children will react to their homecoming. An effective way to deliver this message may be to bring paroled fathers to prison parenting classes to talk about their own experiences. By sharing their stories, guest speakers can help the fathers make realistic plans for building relationships with their children.

One of the topics addressed at length in California parenting classes is domestic violence. This should be central to all prison parenting classes. Studies suggest that children who are abused or who are exposed to violence committed by their fathers against their mothers have severe problems later in life. Females disproportionately become involved with men who abuse them, and males disproportionately batter their partners (Gelles and Straus 1988; Dobash and Dobash 1979). In California, it is not known what percentage of young men on parole have been convicted of domestic violence, because the CYA has only recently begun to separate domestic violence from general assault in their records. We should soon have a better idea of what percentage of men are sent to the CYA on domestic violence charges. The criminal records of the paroled fathers in this study show that just over 3 percent were convicted of crimes against children (molestation, abuse, neglect). While some of these men may be legally required to avoid contact with their children once they are released, some will not. Prison is one of the few places where we can force these men to confront domestic violence issues and present them with alternative responses to anger and frustration.

While I believe that parenting classes can be extremely useful for young fathers, one caveat should be noted. Classes that are hastily prepared are likely to have little positive effect on fathering attitudes and behavior. The CYA uses a comprehensive and standardized curriculum that has been developed to meet the needs of the population. It is essential that states and nonprofits interested in presenting parenting classes carefully research and plan the material they present.

Help Children Visit Incarcerated Fathers

Inmates in CYA institutions are allowed to see their children at least once every two weeks. However, most see their children far less often. As described, 33 percent of the paroled fathers reported that they did not see their children at all during their incarceration, and 22 percent saw them only once or twice. These low levels of visitation should be of concern given evidence, both from this project and from the literature, of positive benefits associated with parent/child visitation in prison.

In her work with children of incarcerated parents, Johnson (1995) found that parent/child separation has numerous negative effects on children. Some of these effects include depression, anger, guilt, and academic problems. While social workers and incarcerated parents sometimes fear prison visitation will cause further problems for children, Johnson found that this is not the case. Half of the children in her study who visited their parents in prison had short-term behavioral reactions (hyperactivity or excitability), but these reactions usually lasted less than a week. She found no evidence of any long-term negative effects from prison visitation. Johnson argues that at least four benefits result from parent/child visitation in prison:

- Visits allow children to express their emotional reactions to the separation, which they may not be allowed to do elsewhere.
- Visitation allows parents to work out their feelings about separation and loss, and therefore helps them become better able to help their children with the same issues.
- Visitation allows children to see their parents realistically. Parent-child separation normally produces irrational feelings and fears within children about their parents; children also entertain unrealistic fantasies when they have no contact with their parent. Visits allow children to release these feelings, fears,

and fantasies and to replace them with a more realistic understanding of their parents' characteristics and circumstances.

• Visits allow parents to model appropriate interactions for children who react inappropriately, but understandably, to the circumstances of separation. This is particularly important for children who do not accept their new caregivers and/or whose reactive behaviors are difficult to manage.

While Johnson's work suggests that prison visitation may be highly beneficial for children, I believe that it may be helpful for fathers as well. The parolees talked at length about how they looked forward to visits with their children while they were incarcerated. These visits allowed them to feel connected and involved in the children's lives. While I do not have any direct evidence for this, prison visits may also help men develop more realistic expectations for their homecoming to their children.

Because prison visitation appears to be positive for both fathers and their children, steps should be taken to encourage it. One of the most obvious ways to accomplish this is to place men in prisons close to their children's hometown. As described in chapter 2, transportation is a major factor limiting the number of times inmates see their children. In California, juvenile inmates can be placed in prisons anywhere in the state. Policies such as these should be reconsidered.

Given the realities of the prison system, there may be times when placing fathers near their children is not feasible. When this happens, more transportation services need to be made available to families. This is particularly true when prisons are located far from public transportation lines. Requiring that the state or county provide transportation may not be possible economically, but the nonprofit groups that currently provide transportation at some facilities should be encouraged and helped to expand their services, perhaps with some funding from the state. These transportation services are crucial. At one prison's visiting hall I overheard a woman mention how many hours it had taken her to get there. She had traveled halfway across the state by train but could not find public transportation from the train station to the prison. She finally discovered that a nonprofit group offered rides from the train station. Had these services not existed, she would not have been able to see her son.

A final way to help children visit prisons is to carefully evaluate lockdown procedures in prisons. In chapter 2, I described how families sometimes arrived at the prison only to be denied admittance because the inmate they wanted to visit was on "lockdown." Lockdowns are clearly necessary to protect prison guards, potential visitors, and the inmates themselves. In these cases, however, prison officials should make a strong effort to contact families who are planning to visit, especially those traveling any distance. It is likely that families who have a bad experience, such as being denied admittance to the prison, will be unwilling to return lest the same thing happen again. If families are contacted, they may be more willing to make trips to the prison in the future.

A difficult question raised by proposals to facilitate visiting between inmates and their children involves the desirability of encouraging criminals to be involved with their children. Some might argue that these men, given their pasts, are unsuitable fathers and should be kept away from their children. While it is important to acknowledge that some inmates have committed serious crimes, the data from this project indicate that a fairly substantial percentage are capable of high levels of consistent and positive involvement with their children. This involvement can be beneficial for everyone. Prison visitation allows men to build relationships with children in a supervised setting. Of course, children should never be forced to visit their fathers, and children's guardians must be allowed to make the final decision about visitation. But when all parties are in agreement, every effort should be made to facilitate visits.

Make Visiting Hours Child-Friendly

Once children arrive at the prison, they should be made as comfortable as possible. As described, many incarcerated fathers have little experience with children and do not know how to play with them or keep them entertained. The fact that there are no toys or activities available during prison visiting hours complicates their efforts to interact with their children. Prisons should consider installing swing sets, slides, sandboxes, and other play areas. Prisons should also provide toys for use during visits. In California, several prisons in the juvenile system have swing sets available during visiting hours. Inmates told me that the swings were one of the most important ways they interacted with their children.

Prisons should also consider allowing fathers to take pictures with their children. Not all prisons in the CYA system allow cameras. I asked Marco, who had served his time at a prison that did not allow it, how the CYA could improve visiting hours.

> Maybe pictures. You know, my girlfriend tried to bring a camera one time and they like to show friends or whatever pictures of your kids, but it looks better when you're in it, you know. Look at the picture I just took of my daughter or son out there. You know, a picture . . . by the sandbox, a big ol' pile of sand or something, you know, you guys doing something together, or smiling, or you making him smile.

Taking a picture with a child is fun, and it provides a keepsake for both fathers and children. A father can hang up the picture in his dormitory and show it to his friends. Pictures allow children to remember their father and the time they spent together at the prison.

House Fathers Separately and Expand Phone Privileges

Incarcerated fathers can be a source of support for each other. Many of the in-depth interview respondents talked about how important it was to gather together with other fathers so that they could talk about their children. They said, however, that talking about children was much more difficult around men who were not fathers. Nonfathers frequently treated such talk as a sign of weakness and ridiculed it. I asked Kevin if he thought the other inmates in the prison were supportive of him as a father.

> Sometimes, if you find another father who loves their kids and, you know, misses their kids, yeah. But the guys without kids really don't, you know. They still might talk about a nephew or something, but it's not the same thing as meeting somebody who has a kid. They're trying to be a good dad, too, or missing their children. You connect better with them, and they're supportive more with each other.

Because incarcerated fathers can find support from other fathers, it makes sense to set aside dormitories, or sections of dormitories, that are specifically reserved for them. This would make it easier for fathers to share problems and experiences with others in a similar situation. It would also be easier to provide these men with ongoing parenting classes and support groups.

Another advantage to having special living quarters for fathers is that father-specific policies can exist which might, in a mixed environment, be perceived as special privileges and thereby create tensions among inmates. I am referring particularly to the suspension of strict phone regulations when calling children. Many incarcerated men feel alienated from their children because they see them and speak to them so infrequently. Increasing phone privileges to at least twice a week would enable them to build and maintain relationships with their children. When I asked Charles how the CYA could improve conditions for fathers, he explained how expanded phone privileges could have helped him:

> They could allow more phone time to at least call them, you know, to talk to them. Like sometimes during the week, I'll get a letter like "your daughter's been acting up," and you're not able to call her, and sometimes if you call her and talk to her, let her hear your voice, it could ease a lot of tension. That's just what she's going through. It's a lot that . . . I think my daughter will be missing without me there. She sees I'm not there, so she puts a lot of frustration on her mother, too. If I'm able to talk to her a couple of times a week . . . she'd be more comfortable.

Increasing phone privileges would allow men to participate more actively in the daily lives of their children. Of course, such a policy is not without its problems. It would require that prison staff monitor phone calls to ensure that the fathers are calling their children and not other people. Because men in prison can only make collect calls, such a policy would also require the consent of the children's caretakers.

One of the criticisms that is likely to be raised about the suggestion that fathers be given more phone access involves the purpose of the prison. Should prison be for punishment or for rehabilitation? Today, the public is demanding a prison system designed around punishment. This emphasis on punishment is likely to engender resistance to policies that appear to help incarcerated inmates build or maintain relationships with their children. Such policies may appear to offer special privileges that negate the punishment aspect of prison. The problem with this view is that policies which strengthen father/child relationships do not simply benefit the inmate father; they can also benefit families and communities. For this reason, helping inmates build relationships with their children is not a matter of extending special privileges. Instead, it is about mitigating the societal harm resulting from their incarceration.

Share Information between the Prison and Child Support Systems

One of the problems men face when they return home from prison is that they owe money for child support. As described in chapter 3, men are not legally responsible for this support while they are in prison. In practice, however, the system continues to charge them. The men often do not have the knowledge or the self-confidence to contest this alleged debt. In order to prevent the erroneous charges from being made in the first place, an information link needs to be established between county child support collection bodies and the prison. Once a man enters the system, child support agencies need to be notified and the man's obligations should be temporarily suspended. On his release, these obligations must resume. The enforcement authorities need to be encouraged to work with the parolee and his parole agent to develop a sensible plan for fulfilling his child support obligations.

Policy Recommendations for Outside the Prison

While we develop policies to aid incarcerated fathers, it is important to address issues affecting young fathers in the community, both those who have been incarcerated and those who have not. Nonprofit corporations and public agencies have developed policies and educational campaigns to encourage young men to take responsibility for their children. While the primary goal is usually to increase the amount of child support the men pay, some groups try to encourage fathers to be more involved with their children. Because little is known about the factors associated with active fatherhood, these policies are often based on questionable assumptions about the attitudes and behaviors of young fathers. All too often they have as their centerpiece the idea that men either do not want to be involved with their children or do not understand the responsibilities that fatherhood entails. For example, child support laws that force fathers to make payments through the state are based on the assumption that men actively resist supporting children. In contrast, the California billboard campaign "Being a Father Means Being There" is based on the idea that fathers simply need a reminder to encourage involvement with their children.

After interviewing paroled fathers, it became clear to me that they are aware of the responsibilities associated with parenthood and that most are willing to try to be "good fathers." Other researchers working in the general population of young fathers have reached similar conclusions (Allen and Doherty 1996; Furstenberg 1995; Rivara, Sweeney, and Henderson 1986; Wattenberg 1993). This project provides evidence that fathers fail to live up to their responsibilities for reasons that are far more complicated than intentions or lack of knowledge. Because of this complexity, it will take more than punitive laws or catchy billboards to increase men's involvement. What follows are recommendations for public policies that could encourage a young man's formal and informal participation with his family.

Move Away from a Deficit Model of Fathering

The "deficit model" of adolescent fatherhood assumes that young men are not interested in or able to fulfill the cultural expectations of this role (Rhoden and Robinson 1997). All young fathers are seen as immature, uninterested in active participation with their children, and unable to support the children financially. Without denying the existence of adolescent fathers who do fit this description, it is important that we not assume it is true for all young men. As Rhoden and Robinson (1997) point out, a deficit perspective can become a self-fulfilling prophecy. They comment, "This deficit perspective on young fathers excludes them from involvement in parenting from the start. Professionals who carry this mind-set are guided unwittingly in ways that exclude and demean young men from any involvement" (108). When we start with the assumption that fathers will be actively involved with their children, we allow young men the opportunity to step up to the role.

Develop Strong Social Support Networks for Fathers

A young father's family and friends play an important role in encouraging or discouraging his involvement with his children. When a man has a strong social network that supports his participation with his child, he is far more likely to be involved. The opposite is also true. When a man tries to build a relationship with his child but encounters hostility or disapproval from his family, friends, or child's mother, he is unlikely to maintain his level of effort. Given research showing the importance of these relationships in the general population of young fathers (DeLuccie 1995; Danziger 1987; Furstenberg 1995; Stack 1974), it would be useful to develop policies to help all young fathers build and maintain such ties. Such a goal, however, is particularly important for parolees who may have damaged their relationships during the period of their incarceration.

Developing public policies to strengthen family and friend relationships is not an easy matter. Because these social network ties are complex and private, they are difficult to manipulate through policy. Some limited actions are available to us, however. First, it is important that all services provided to young fathers involve members of their social network. As a result of the recent upsurge in interest in young fatherhood, various states, localities, and non-profit groups are creating classes and support groups to aid young fathers. These programs should be designed to include both the families of the men and the mothers of their children. The California Youth Authority, in its parole parenting classes, has experienced success with its policy of including family members. In an evaluation of the classes, we observed that "the attendance of a man's significant others is extremely useful for helping parolees build strong relationships with their wives and girlfriends and in establishing a good classroom environment" (Cohen et al. 1997).

A second way to strengthen social networks is by teaching communication skills to young fathers and to the mothers of their children. Poor communication between parents is one reason these men limit contact with their children. My observations in parenting classes suggest that, like most adolescents, young paroled fathers simply do not have the communication skills to maintain a successful relationship with the mother of their children. I suspect that the mothers' communication skills are not any more advanced. I include a quote from the evaluation report of the parole parenting classes to illustrate how teaching basic communication skills can help young fathers:

> A number of students indicated that the classes helped them communicate with their partners. One young man told us that he liked to read in

his workbook and show things to his girlfriend. He was often surprised how relevant it was to their relationship. Pointing to a page about expressing love in his workbook, he said, "I showed her this . . . and I told her that when we argue, 'It's not that I don't love you or nothing. It's not that. Read this and you'll understand.'" Echoing the sentiments of a number of students, one parolee commented that he learned to cool off before arguments happen. He said, "When my girlfriend's mad, I don't go like [yells]. I just let her cool down. I go for a walk or walk to the store and come back later. And if I see that she's calm, then I'll talk about whatever problem we had. Like that." Another young man said, "The teachers kind of teach you how to compromise. . . . You know, like when parents get frustrated. One's tired, and let's say both of them are tired, they don't want to take care of the kid. They need to talk it out, take turns or something." (Cohen et al. 1997)

Teaching parents healthy ways to communicate may help them maintain amicable relationships. In turn, these amicable relationships can facilitate men's involvement with their children.

Implement New Policies to Strengthen a Father's Legal Ties to His Children

Public officials have attempted to increase the rate of paternity establishment, child support order establishment, and child support compliance. To date, however, they have not been highly successful. To increase their success, changes should be made. First, they should design campaigns to increase paternity establishment with an emphasis on young men's rights as fathers, not just their responsibilities. My observations in parenting classes suggest that young fathers already understand that legal fatherhood entails responsibilities. In contrast, they do not know that declaring paternity will confer certain rights. Wattenberg's work with young fathers (1993) confirms my observation that men are unaware of the benefits of paternity.

All young fathers should be informed that, by declaring paternity, they make their child eligible for their Social Security, armed services, health care, and workers' compensation benefits. They should also be told that paternity establishment allows them to advocate legally for their children and to request formal visitation privileges or custody. This is important information for young fathers because many have problems seeing their children due to conflicts with the mothers. Legal visitation rights may be an attractive option for them.

There are several ways that we can educate young fathers about paternity establishment. The first is to provide them with information at the hospital when their babies are born. This information could also be presented in parenting classes, high school sex education courses, and support groups. At the same time, it would be useful to design a public education campaign around the theme of paternity establishment. Central to all of these efforts, however, must be the idea that legal fatherhood is a coupling of rights and responsibilities; it is not simply a way to force fathers to pay child support.

In addition to emphasizing fatherhood rights, we need to make sure that the legal responsibilities attached to fatherhood are simplified and standardized. In the previous section, I discussed changes in the child support system for incarcerated men, but changes also need to be made for men who have not been incarcerated. My research indicates that the vast majority of young paroled fathers are not legally required to pay child support. While most would be able to pay only minimal support, making an effort to register men with the child support system sends an important message about responsibility and accountability. Alongside efforts to establish more child support orders, we must also make the system more responsive to the needs of fathers. As it stands, it is very difficult for men to get a modification of their child support payments when their circumstances (such as employment or number of dependents) change. It would help these men if the paperwork and process for changing existing orders were streamlined and simplified.

A Final Note

I conducted an in-depth interview with Sam in the spring of 1998. At the time, he was living with his parents and daughter in rural California. He had been out on parole about a year after completing a three-year sentence on a charge of assault with a deadly weapon. Like many of the men I interviewed, he spoke passionately about his belief that the public neither knows nor cares about prisoners and parolees.

> There's a lot of people in there [prison] that actually care about their families and they ain't really bad people, you know. They ain't really bad. A lot of people, unless they're in for murder or whatever, they're not really bad people. They just caught up in the wrong time, wrong situation type of thing. . . . The people in there . . . got heart. They're people, too, you know. Just you don't know their situation unless you live in their shoes. If you haven't walked in their shoes, you don't understand nothing about them.

Other men told me about how they have encountered fear, misconceptions, and stereotyping since their release from prison. Tyrell, a young father living in an inner-city area, talked at great length about this topic.

It's like they think you're just a bad person, you know. They don't really know the person. They need to get to know the person first. Then understand what he's been through, what he's going through, what he's trying to do, you know, before they just put that jacket on 'em, like you're bad, you're locked up, I don't want nothing else to do with you.

The parolees' sense that they are seen as a monolithic group, not as individuals with diverse lives and social contexts, does not come out of the air. Public attention has become increasingly focused on crime, and criminals have come to be seen only in terms of their offenses. When I took a job with the California Youth Authority five years ago, Tyrell and Sam's comments could have described me. I had spent little time thinking about juvenile criminals as people, much less as fathers. Over the course of this project, I met many young men who, while they identified as criminals, also felt that their father identity was central to who they were.

The men I encountered expressed deep concerns about the effects of prison on their fathering. They believed that their experiences in prison had permanently harmed their ability to be involved as parents. The more exposure I had to their lives, the more convinced I became that the topic of incarcerated fatherhood is a pressing political and social issue. In conclusion, I hope that what I have written will provide a starting point for the discussion of solutions to the myriad problems associated with incarcerated and paroled fatherhood. The fathers introduced in this book are only a small part of a much larger national population of criminal fathers. I hope that their voices and experiences can help us formulate a response to the troubling intersection of young fatherhood and incarceration.

Notes

1. Prison and Fatherhood: Overlapping Social Problems

1. Index crimes include murder and manslaughter, forcible rape, robbery, aggravated assault, burglary, larceny, motor vehicle theft, and arson.
2. For the purposes of analysis throughout this book, I categorized the thirteen men who reported being of multiracial origins as follows: Latino/white as Latino, Latino/black as black, and white/black as black.

2. Fathering from Behind Bars

1. All reported differences between groups throughout this book are statistically significant at the .05 level unless otherwise noted.

3. Coming Home

1. Controlling for child age decreases these differences between groups only slightly. The difference between whites and blacks remains statistically significant at the .05 level.
2. The difference between generations is significant at the .10 level. While this significance level is not conventionally used by sociologists, I employ it here because of the small number of respondents.

4. **Negotiating Relationships:**
   Paroled Fathers, Families, and Friends

1. Part of this difference can be explained by the different average ages of the white, black, and Latino children, but the difference remains statistically significant even when child age is controlled (data not shown).

2. These differences remain statistically significant even when child age is controlled (data not shown).

Works Cited

Abeyratne, S., B. Sowards, and L. Brewer. 1995. *Youths Incarcerated in ODYS Institutions Who Have Children and Youths Incarcerated in ODYS Institutions Who Are Children of Teenage Parents.* Columbus: Ohio Department of Youth Services, Office of Research.

Allen, W. D., and W. J. Doherty. 1996. The Responsibilities of Fatherhood as Perceived by African American Teenage Fathers. *Families in Society: Journal of Contemporary Human Services* 77(3):142–55.

Anderson, E. 1990. *Streetwise: Race, Class, and Change in an Urban Community.* Chicago: University of Chicago Press.

Arendell, T. 1995. *Fathers and Divorce.* Thousand Oaks, Calif.: Sage.

Austin, J., B. Krisberg, R. DeComo, S. Rudenstein, and D. Del Rosario. 1995. *Juveniles Taken into Custody: Fiscal Year 1993 Statistics Report.* Washington, D.C.: Office of Juvenile Justice and Delinquency Prevention.

Bailey, W. T. 1994. A Longitudinal Study of Fathers' Involvement with Young Children: Infancy to Age Five Years. *Journal of Genetic Psychology* 155(3): 331–39.

Bakker, L. J., B. A. Morris, and L. M. Janus. 1978. Hidden Victims of Crime. *Social Work* 23:143–48.

Bartollas, C., W. J. Miller, and S. Dinitz. 1976. *Juvenile Victimization: The Institutional Paradox.* New York: Wiley.

Belsky, J., L. Youngblade, M. Rovine, and B. Volling. 1991. Patterns of Marital

Change and Parent-Child Interaction. *Journal of Marriage and the Family* 53:487–98.

Bernard, T. J. 1992. *The Cycle of Juvenile Justice.* New York: Oxford University Press.

Bishop, D. M., and C. E. Frazier. 1996. Race Effects in Juvenile Justice Decision-Making: Findings of a Statewide Analysis. *Journal of Criminal Law and Criminology* 86(2):392–414.

Bortner, M. A., and L. M. Williams. 1997. *Youth in Prison: We the People of Unit Four.* New York: Routledge.

Brody, G. H., A. D. Pillegrini, and I. E. Sigel. 1986. Marital Quality and Mother-Child and Father-Child Interactions with School-aged Children. *Developmental Psychology* 22(3):291–96.

California Department of Finance. 1998. *1992–1996 Population: 1970–1996 Race/Ethnic Population Estimates by County with Age and Sex Detail.* Sacramento: Department of Finance. Available from dhs.cahwnet.gov/org/hisp/chs/OHIR/Population/populationindex.htm.

California Youth Authority. 1995. *Office of Criminal Justice Planning Juvenile Justice and Delinquency Prevention Program Project Summary.* Sacramento: Research Division, Ward Information and Parole Research Bureau.

———. 1996. *Characteristics of CYA Population.* Sacramento: Research Division, Ward Information and Parole Research Bureau.

Carroll, L. 1974. *Hacks, Blacks, and Cons: Race Relations in a Maximum Security Prison.* Prospect Heights, Ill.: Waveland Press.

Cazanave, N. 1979. Middle-Income Black Fathers: An Analysis of the Provider Role. *Family Coordinator* 28:583–93.

Christmon, K., and I. Lucky. 1994. Is Early Fatherhood Associated with Alcohol and Other Drug Use? *Journal of Substance Abuse* 6:337–43.

Cohen, L. E., D. Felmlee, A. Nurse, and S. Will. 1997. *Second Year Report to the California Youth Authority: Positive Parenting Program.* Sacramento: California Office of Criminal Justice Planning.

Conley, D. J. 1994. Adding Color to a Black-and-White Picture: Using Qualitative Data to Explain Racial Disproportionality in the Juvenile Justice System. *Journal of Research in Crime and Delinquency* 31(2):135–48.

Connell, R. W. 1990. The State, Gender, and Sexual Politics: Theory and Appraisal. *Theory and Society* 19(4):507–44.

———. 1992. The Big Picture: Masculinities in Recent World History. Unpublished paper.

———. 1995. *Masculinities*. Berkeley: University of California Press.

Corley, D. 2001. Prison Friendships. In *Prison Masculinities,* ed. D. Sabo, T. A. Kupers, and W. London. Philadelphia: Temple University Press.

Cramer, J. C., and K. B. McDonald. 1996. Kin Support and Family Stress: Two Sides to Early Childbearing and Support Networks. *Human Organization* 55(2):160–69.

Daly, K. 1987. Structure and Practice of Familial-based Justice in a Criminal Court. *Law and Society Review* 21:267–89.

———. 1993. Reshaping Fatherhood: Finding the Models. *Journal of Family Issues* 14(4):510–30.

Danziger, S. K. 1987. *Father Involvement in Welfare Families Headed by Adolescent Mothers*. Discussion Paper 856-87. Madison, WI: Institute for Research on Poverty.

Danziger, S. K., and A. Nichols-Casebolt. 1990. Child Support in Paternity Cases. *Social Service Review* 64:458–74.

Darroch, J. E., D. J. Landry, and S. Oslak. 1999. Pregnancy Rates among U.S. Women and Their Partners in 1994. *Family Planning Perspectives* 31(3):122–26.

Davis, A. 1992. Men's Imprisonment: The Financial Cost to Women and Children. In *Prisoners' Children: What Are the Issues?* ed. R. Shaw, 74–85. London: Routledge.

DeLuccie, M. F. 1995. Mothers as Gatekeepers: A Model of Maternal Mediators of Father Involvement. *Journal of Genetic Psychology* 156(1):115–31.

DiNitto, D. D. 1995. *Social Welfare: Politics and Public Policy.* 4th ed. Boston: Allyn and Bacon.

Dobash, R. E., and R. Dobash. 1979. *Violence against Wives: A Case against the Patriarchy*. New York: Free Press.

Edin, K. 2000. What Do Low-Income Single Mothers Say about Marriage? *Social Problems* 47:112–33.

Ekland-Olson, S., M. Supancic, J. Campbell, and K. J. Lenihan. 1983. Postrelease Depression and the Importance of Familial Support. *Criminology* 21(2):253–75.

Elder, G. H., and A. M. O'Rand. 1995. Adult Lives in a Changing Society. In

Sociological Perspectives on Social Psychology, ed. K. S. Cook, G. A. Fine, and J. S. House, 452–75. Boston: Allyn and Bacon.

Elster, A. B., and M. E. Lamb. 1986. Parental Behavior of Adolescent Mothers and Fathers. In *Adolescent Fatherhood,* ed. A. B. Elster and M. E. Lamb. Hillsdale, N.J.: L. Erlbaum.

Elster, A. B., M. E. Lamb, and J. Tavare. 1987. Association between Behavioral and School Problems and Fatherhood in a National Sample of Adolescent Youths. *Journal of Pediatrics* 111:932–36.

Ferraro, K. J., J. M. Johson, S. R. Jorgensen, and F. G. Bolton. 1983. Problems of Prisoners' Families: The Hidden Costs of Imprisonment. *Journal of Family Issues* 4:575–91.

Fine, G. A. 1987. *With the Boys: Little League Baseball and Preadolescent Culture.* Chicago: University of Chicago Press.

Fowler, F. J., Jr. 1995. *Improving Survey Questions: Design and Evaluation.* Thousand Oaks, Calif.: Sage.

Fritsch, T. A., and Burkhead, J. D. 1981. Behavioral Reactions of Children to Parental Absence Due to Imprisonment. *Family Relations* 30:83–88.

Furstenberg, F. F., Jr. 1995. Fathering in the Inner City: Paternal Participation and Public Policy. In *Fatherhood: Contemporary Theory, Research, and Social Policy*, ed. W. Marsiglio, 119–47. Thousand Oaks, Calif.: Sage.

Furstenberg, F. F., Jr., J. Brooks-Gunn, and S. P. Morgan. 1987. *Adolescent Mothers in Later Life.* Cambridge: Cambridge University Press.

Furstenberg, F. F., Jr., K. E. Sherwood, and M. L. Sullivan. 1992, July. *Caring and Paying: What Fathers and Mothers Say about Child Support.* San Francisco: Manpower Demonstration Research Corporation.

Gelles, R. J., and M. A. Straus. 1988. *Intimate Violence.* New York: Simon and Schuster.

Goffman, E. 1961. *Asylums: Essays on the Social Situation of Mental Patients and Other Inmates.* New York: Doubleday.

Hairston, C. F. 1995. Fathers in Prison. In *Children of Incarcerated Parents,* ed. K. Gabel and D. Johnston, 31–40. New York: Lexington Books.

Hale, D. C. 1988. The Impact of Mothers' Incarceration on the Family System: Research and Recommendations. *Deviance and the Family* 12(1–2):143–54.

Holzer, H. 1996. *What Employers Want: Job Prospects for Less-Educated Workers.* New York: Russell Sage Foundation.

Hughes, M. 1998. Turning Points in the Lives of Young Inner-City Men Forgoing Destructive Criminal Behaviors: A Qualitative Study. *Social Work Research* 22(3):143–51.

Huizinga, D., and D. Elliot, 1987. Juvenile Offenders: Prevalence, Offender Incidence, and Arrest Rates by Race. *Crime and Delinquency* 33:206–23.

Hunter, E. J. 1986. Families of Prisoners of War Held in Vietnam: A Seven-Year Study. *Evaluation and Program Planning* 9:243–51.

International Network for Children and Families. 1994. *Redirecting Children's Behavior Workbook*. Gainesville, Fla.

Johnston, D. 1995. Jailed Mothers. In *Children of Incarcerated Parents*, ed. K. Gabel and D. Johnston, 41–58. New York: Lexington Books.

Johnston, D., and K. Gabel. 1995. Incarcerated Parents. In *Children of Incarcerated Parents*, ed. K. Gabel and D. Johnston, 3–20. New York: Lexington Books.

Lareau, A. 2000. My Wife Can Tell Me Who I Know: Methodological and Conceptual Problems in Studying Fathers. *Qualitative Sociology* 23(4):407–33.

Lerman, R. I. 1993. A National Profile of Young Unwed Fathers. In *Young Unwed Fathers: Changing Roles and Emerging Policies,* ed. R. I. Lerman and T. J. Ooms, 27–51. Philadelphia: Temple University Press.

Lerman, R. I., and T. J. Ooms. 1993. *Young Unwed Fathers: Changing Roles and Emerging Policies*. Philadelphia: Temple University Press.

McCubin, H. I., B. B. Dahl, G. R. Lester, and B. A. Ross. 1975. The Returned Prisoner of War: Factors in Family Reintegration. *Journal of Marriage and the Family* 37(3):471–78.

McDermott, K., and R. D. King. 1992. Prison Rule 102: 'Stand By Your Man': The Impact of Penal Policy on the Families of Prisoners. In *Prisoners' Children: What Are the Issues?* ed. R. Shaw, 50–73. London: Routledge.

McKenry, P. C., S. J. Price, M. A. Fine, and J. Serovich. 1992. Predictors of Single, Noncustodial Fathers' Physical Involvement with Their Children. *Journal of Genetic Psychology* 153(3):305–19.

Mauer, M., and T. Huling. 1995. *Young Black Americans and the Criminal Justice System: Five Years Later.* Washington, D.C.: Sentencing Project.

Messerschmidt, J. W. 1993. *Masculinities and Crime: Critique and Reconceptualization of Theory.* Lanham, MD: Rowman and Littlefield.

Mirandé, A. 1991. Ethnicity and Fatherhood. In *Fatherhood and Families in Cul-*

tural Context, ed. F. W. Bozett and S. M. H. Hanson, 53–82. New York: Springer.

Moore, K. A. 1995, September. *Executive Summary: Report to Congress on Out-of-Wedlock Childbearing.* DHHS Pub. No. (PHS) 95-1257-1. Hyattsville, MD: Department of Health and Human Services.

Mott, F. L. 1990. When Is a Father Really Gone? Paternal-Child Contact in Father-Absent Homes. *Demography* 27(4):499–517.

Newton, C. 1994. Gender Theory and Prison Sociology: Using Theories of Masculinities to Interpret the Sociology of Prisons for Men. *Howard Journal* 33(3):193–202.

Office of Juvenile Justice and Delinquency Prevention. 1999. *OJJDP Statistical Briefing Book. Online.* Available from ojjdp.ncjrs.org/ojstatbb/qa162.html. 30 September.

Parent, D. G., V. Leiter, S. Kennedy, L. Livens, D. Wentworth, and S. Wilcox. 1994. *Conditions of Confinement: Juvenile Detention and Corrections Facilities: Research Summary.* Washington, D.C.: Office of Juvenile Justice and Delinquency Prevention.

Pirog-Good, M. A., and D. H. Good. 1995. Child Support Enforcement for Teenage Fathers: Problems and Prospects. *Journal of Policy Analysis and Management* 14(1):25–42.

Rhoden, J. L., and B. E. Robinson. 1997. Teen Dads: A Generative Fathering Perspective versus the Deficit Myth. In *Generative Fathering: Beyond Deficit Perspectives,* ed. A. J. Hawkins and D. C. Dollahite, 105–17. Thousand Oaks, Calif.: Sage.

Rindfuss, R. R., C. G. Swicegood, and R. A. Rosenfeld. 1987. Disorder in the Life Course: How Common and Does It Matter? *American Sociological Review* 52:785–801.

Rivara, F. P., P. J. Sweeney, and B. F. Henderson. 1986. Black Teenage Fathers: What Happens When the Child Is Born? *Pediatrics* 78(1):151–58.

Roy, K. 1999. Low-Income Single Fathers in an African American Community and the Requirements of Welfare Reform. *Journal of Family Issues* 20(4):432–57.

Sabo, D., T. A. Kupers, and W. London. 2001. Gender and the Politics of Punishment. In *Prison Masculinities*, ed. D. Sabo, T. A. Kupers, and W. London, 3–18. Philadelphia: Temple University Press.

Sampson, R. J., and J. H. Laub. 1993. *Crime in the Making: Pathways and Turning Points through Life.* Cambridge: Harvard University Press.

Schlossman, S. 1995. Delinquent Children: The Juvenile Reform School. In *The Oxford History of the Prison: The Practice of Punishment in Western Society,* eds. N. Morris and D. J. Rothman, 363–89. New York: Oxford University Press.

Schuldberg, D., and S. Guisinger. 1991. Divorced Fathers Describe Their Former Wives: Devaluation and Contrast. In *Women and Divorce /Men and Divorce: Gender Differences in Separation, Divorce, and Remarriage,* ed. S. S. Volgy, 61–88. New York: Haworth Press.

Schuman, H., and G. Kalton. 1985. Survey Methods. In *Handbook of Social Psychology: Vol. 1. Theory and Method,* 3d ed., ed. G. Lindzey and E. Aronson, 635–97. New York: Random House.

Scott, E. S., and T. Grisso. 1997. The Evolution of Adolescence: A Developmental Perspective on Juvenile Justice Reform. *Journal of Criminal Law and Criminology* 88:137–89.

Segal, L. 1990. S*low Motion: Changing Masculinities, Changing Men.* New Brunswick, N.J.: Rutgers University Press.

Seltzer, J. A., and Y. Brandreth. 1994. What Fathers Say about Involvement with Children after Separation. *Journal of Family Issues* 15(1):49–77.

Sickmund, M., H. N. Snyder, and E. Poe-Yamagata. 1997. *Juvenile Offenders and Victims: 1997 Update on Violence.* Washington, D.C.: Office of Juvenile Justice and Delinquency Prevention.

Stack, C. B. 1974. *All Our Kin: Strategies for Survival in a Black Community.* New York: Harper and Row.

Stouthamer-Loeber, M., and E. H. Wei. 1998. The Precursors of Young Fatherhood and Its Effect on Delinquency of Teenage Males. *Journal of Adolescent Health* 22:56–65.

Suarez-Orozco, C., and M. Suarez-Orozco. 1995. *Transformations: Migration, Family Life, and Achievement Motivation among Latino Adolescents.* Stanford: Stanford University Press.

Sullivan, M. L. 1993. Young Fathers and Parenting in Two Inner-City Neighborhoods. In *Young Unwed Fathers: Changing Roles and Emerging Policies,* ed. R. I. Lerman and T. J. Ooms, 52–73. Philadelphia: Temple University Press.

Sykes, G. M. 1958. *The Society of Captives: A Study of a Maximum Security Prison*. Princeton: Princeton University Press.

Teachman, J. D. 1991. Contributions to Children by Divorced Fathers. *Social Problems* 38(3):358–71.

Teti, D. M., and M. E. Lamb. 1986. Sex-Role Learning and Adolescent Fatherhood. In *Adolescent Fatherhood*, eds. A. B. Elster and M. E. Lamb, 19–30. Hillsdale, N.J.: Erlbaum.

Thornberry, T. P., E. H. Wei, M. Stouthamer-Loeber, and J. Van Dyke. 2000, January. Teenage Fatherhood and Delinquent Behavior. Washington, D.C.: Office of Juvenile Justice and Delinquency Prevention.

Tittle, C. R. 1972. *Society of Subordinates: Inmate Organization in a Narcotics Hospital*. Bloomington: Indiana University Press.

Toch, H. 1992. *Living in Prison: The Ecology of Survival*. Rev. ed. Washington, D.C.: American Psychological Association.

U.S. Bureau of the Census. 1992, September. *Census of Population and Housing: Summary Tape File 3A* (CD90-3A)(CDROM). Washington, D.C.

U.S. House Committee on Ways and Means. 1993. *Overview of Entitlement Programs, 1993 Green Book*. Washington, D.C.: Government Printing Office.

Ventura, S. J., J. A. Martin, S. C. Curtin, F. Menacker, and B. E. Hamilton. 2001. *Births: Final Data for 1999*. National Vital Statistics Reports 49(1). Hyattsville, MD: National Center for Health Statistics.

Waller, M. R. 1995, August. *Claiming Fatherhood: Paternity, Culture, and Public Policy*. Paper presented at the annual meeting of the American Sociological Association, Washington, D.C.

Walters, L. H., and S. F. Chapman. 1991. Changes in Legal Views of Parenthood: Implications for Fathers in Minority Cultures. In *Fatherhood and Families in Cultural Context*, ed. F. W. Bozett and S. M. H. Hanson, 83–113. New York: Springer.

Wattenberg, E. 1993. Paternity Actions and Young Fathers. In *Young Unwed Fathers: Changing Roles and Emerging Policies*, eds. R. I. Lerman and T. J. Ooms, 213–34. Philadelphia: Temple University Press.

Wattenberg, E., R. Brewer, and M. Resnick. 1991. *A Study of Paternity Decisions of Young, Unmarried Parents*. Report submitted to the Ford Foundation. Minneapolis: Center for Urban and Regional Affairs, University of Minnesota.

Wilson, W. J. 1996. *When Work Disappears: The World of the New Urban Poor.* New York: Knopf.

Wordes, M., T. S. Bynum, and C. J. Corley. 1994. Locking Up Youth: The Impact of Race on Detention Decisions. *Journal of Research in Crime and Delinquency* 31:149–65.

Zayas, L. H., S. P. Schinke, and D. Casareno. 1987. Hispanic Adolescent Fathers: At Risk and Underresearched. *Children and Youth Services Review* 9:235–48.

Index